To
Peter & Irene,

Keep fit — have fun.

Barrie

Life's A Lottery
Or Is It?

Life's A Lottery
Or Is It?

by

BARRIE C. JOHNSTON, OBE

The Memoir Club

© Barrie C. Johnston OBE 2001

First published in 2001 by
The Memoir Club
Whitworth Hall
Spennymoor
County Durham

All rights reserved.
Unauthorised duplication
contravenes existing laws.

British Library Cataloguing in
Publication Data.
A catalogue record for this book
is available from the
British Library.

ISBN: 1 84104 028 2

Typeset by George Wishart & Associates, Whitley Bay.
Printed by Bookcraft (Bath) Ltd.

*To my dear wife Cynthia
and to our children, Nicola and John,
and their respective families*

Contents

List of Illustrations ix
Acknowledgements xi
Preface xiii

Part I: Early Years

Chapter 1	Growing Up	3
Chapter 2	The Run-Up to World War II	12
Chapter 3	The Royal Marines	23

Part II: A Career in Merchant Banking

Chapter 1	Back to Merchant Banking: Helbert Wagg/Schroder Wagg	37
Chapter 2	Charterhouse	59

Part III: Work with Charities

Chapter 1	Involvement with Charities	79
Chapter 2	Charities Aid Foundation	81
Chapter 3	Royal Marines Association	91
Chapter 4	Royal Marines Corps Funds	95
Chapter 5	Royal Marines Museum	97
Chapter 6	King George's Fund for Sailors	105
Chapter 7	Barnardo's	113
Chapter 8	The Chartered Institute of Management Accountants	119
Chapter 9	The Worshipful Company of Turners	121
Chapter 10	The Spastics Society (now SCOPE)	126
Chapter 11	The Imperial War Museum	128
Chapter 12	Royal Navy and Royal Marines Dependent Relatives' Fund	132

Chapter 13	SSAFA Forces Help Fund Raising Committee	134
Chapter 14	Royal Agricultural Benevolent Institution	136
Chapter 15	The Royal College of Radiologists	140
Chapter 16	The Ralph Snow Charity	144
Chapter 17	Hearing Dogs for Deaf People	146
Chapter 18	Honour	153
Chapter 19	VE Day Celebrations	156
Chapter 20	The Royal Association for Disability & Rehabilitation (RADAR)	159
Chapter 21	The British Federation of Women Graduates Charitable Foundation	166
Chapter 22	The Royal Electrical & Mechanical Engineers (REME)	168
Chapter 23	The RAF Pathfinder Museum	171
Chapter 24	The Abbeyfield (Cheam) Society	172
Chapter 25	Charities: Conclusion and Future Views	175

Part IV: Your Money – How Not to Lose It!

Chapter 1	Introduction	181
Chapter 2	Inflation – Its Effect on Any Investment	186
Chapter 3	Advice: Who Do You Believe and Where Do You Go?	189
Chapter 4	The Performance of Government Stocks and Equities	201
Chapter 5	Personal Financial Planning	207

Part V: Sport and Family Life

Chapter 1	Sport – Cheam Fields Club	211
Chapter 2	The Family	214

Appendices

Appendix A	UK Cost of Living Index and Other Indices	220
Appendix B	Names and Addresses of Charities and Other Relevant Organizations	227

List of Illustrations

Brother Mick and me, 1929 7
Shoreham Aerodrome, 1915. Father in rear seat of plane 20
My matchstick warships, 1944: HMS *Coventry*, HMS *Dorsetshire*,
  HMS *Kempenfelt*, HMS *Hood* unfinished. All on the same scale . 21
Father, Lieutenant, Royal Flying Corps, 1916 29
Father and me, 1945. I am wearing the same Sam Browne! 29
Father and Mother, 1945 32
Our wedding day, 13th October, 1952 44
Christopher Breach's wedding with Nicola, 1985 45
John's wedding to Christine Hood, 1995 46
Royal Marines Association 'standing easy'. The beginning
  of the Drum Head Service 92
Falkland Islands – 'Reflection' 102
Falkland Islands Stone – Royal Marines Museum
  Memorial Garden 103
HMS *Victory*. King George's Fund for Sailors. Before dinner
  in Admiral Nelson's cabin 110
King George's Fund for Sailors – Reception at the Guildhall.
  Introduction to HM the Queen 111
King George's Fund for Sailors Reception.
  Self (Hon Treasurer), HRH Prince Philip, (President) 111
HRH Princess Diana signing the Visitors' Book at Chester 117
Worshipful Company of Turners: the Mistress and Master
  Turner, 1990 124
The Royal College of Radiologists. Honorary Fellowship,
  1996, with the President, Dr Michael Brindle 142
Investiture Ceremony 1994. (BCA Films Copyright) 154
Cheam Fields Club. The Three Champions, 1950 212
Ballarat, Australia. With the last working goldminer 215

Arches National Park, Utah, USA 215
Alaska. Before canoeing to glacier face 215
Alaska. On a glacier and about to dog-sledge, 1990s.
    Cynthia seated 216

Acknowledgements

I MUCH APPRECIATED the typing of this book by Mrs Ann Crawford of Altrincham, who was so good at interpreting my writing. My sincere thanks go to Sir Peter Baldwin KCB for writing the generous Preface and to my wife Cynthia for putting up with piles of paper in our dining room for five months. She also corrected my grammatical errors!

All the comments about the Charities have been checked by them where possible, to make sure that the facts are correct. The views expressed are mine alone; no one has tried to influence them in any way.

My gratitude is recorded for the permission of Buckingham Palace and BCA Associates Ltd for permission to print the picture of the Investiture and to Mr Bruce Gray for his help in reproducing all the photographs on disc.

The graphs and tables in the closing chapters are printed with the permission of Barclays Capital, who have kept such records for many decades – records which are generally recognized as being totally accurate. These support my views as expressed in the text.

Preface

LIFE, WE FIND, is about the next thing. Next things come so thick and fast that we rarely think about them except to deal with them. But other people's next things can be very interesting. If we take time to hear about them, we are rewarded both by seeing significance in them and by discovering significance in our own. Thank goodness for other people's lives and for ours. Arrival at this point is what this book accomplishes.

Over the centuries in our part of the world, the usefulness of skills has tended to engage people for their working lives in some single institutionalized employment within, for example, a company, a firm, an authority or a school. In present and future times we are told to expect our lives to cohere around our competences rather than a single employment. This book spans these phenomena because Barrie Johnston's competences have taken him into so many situations where he has exercised them, whether within or outside remunerated employment.

A connecting factor emerges from his taking us through those situations in his youth, in the Royal Marines, in the City of London (to which he has been devoted throughout and since his employment there) and concurrently in charities great and small. This is the human aspiration that what is done should be right. Vision of what would be right and the getting of it become the reasons for doing it at all. This is motivation which we, like Barrie, can find even in sport. But 'right' has both technical and moral senses. Both have led Barrie from one situation to the next and produced the sequence of the book's chapters.

After the heat of situations in the earlier chapters comes the cool reflective breeze of expertise, presented in the modest terms of common sense, conveying the essence of his cultivated competence in making money grow. This part of the presentation takes all of Part IV, partly because he charts the many rocks on which savings may founder, including fiscal decisions of Government, and partly because he recognizes that the market which he served in employment provides a poor service when it comes to important advice to people or causes where means are slender. It is typical of his lifelong service to charities, and doubtless in wider personal circles, that he has seen his book as an opportunity to offer practical advice in lucid terms to the uninitiated, inexpert or pre-occupied multitude, for the potential value in money that it may be to them. Including Government, we can all listen with advantage.

Sir Peter Baldwin KCB

Part I

Early Years

CHAPTER ONE

Growing Up

I WAS BORN ON THE 7th August 1925 and my Mother said that that event in our family history began some ten minutes after midnight – this probably accounts for the fact that I have always been able to stay up very late at night and have never had difficulty in getting up early in the morning. In fact, for all of my adult life I have survived on a maximum of no more than six hours or so of sleep every night. Going to bed at 1.00 am has been average, and a late night out to, say, 2.00 am has had little effect on my constitution as far as I can see.

This fortunate ability has been of immense value as the years have progressed, and it has been a useful habit to develop – so many people go to bed early at around 10.00 pm and then say that they sleep badly. I guess this is because they are never really physically or mentally tired. Yet trying to get that message across to others has always failed.

Memory is a funny thing and the writing of this book has helped me to recall some of the odd happenings that occurred to me as a child, the earliest of which is not in fact about my parents, but of a very vivid recollection of the dining room in the flat in Wandsworth Common when, at considerable risk to the state of the crockery, I used to badger my Mother to let me take the plates (one at a time I guess) from the kitchen across the hall and then, on tip-toe, place them on the table. I can only assume that this is so vivid in my mind because I must have dropped one, then been ticked off in no uncertain way for being so clumsy.

Mother was a very fit, tall and elegant lady whose father, born in Hull, had been a sailor. In his early days, in fact, he 'sailed before the mast' around Cape Horn and ended his sea-going days, as Chief Engineer on the Governor of Nigeria's yacht, when he married my maternal grandmother, whose singing ability was considerable. This musical trait was handed down to my mother, who could whistle better than anyone I have ever heard – to my shame, some time at around the age of six or seven, I repeatedly asked her to stop whistling – presumably because I could not do it myself! Mother, in later life, referred to this from time to time, and asked me why I had said 'stop it'. In her usual way she never appeared to hold that against me – she was a very good friend for such a long time, especially early in the war (1939-43), when Father was away for most of the time.

Mother's father, Grandpa Birch, was a formidable man, who always said that you marry either a woman or a ship, and when he married my grandmother, he did leave the sea. He became the director of a small company, not far from the Oval Cricket Ground, called 'Alabastine', and every school holiday for several years, it was a treat to go on the Green Line bus with my Mother and brother to his factory. The product was used to fill cracks in walls and ceilings etc, but it shrank on drying. It was the forerunner of what we know today as Polyfilla, Tetrion etc., the success of which eventually forced the closure of Alabastine. In any case, the whole works, and the men in it, were always coated in white powder and there is no way in which this would have been tolerated under today's health and safety rules.

On many Sundays, my grandparents would come by train to lunch in Cheam and after a meal of large joints of meat and big puddings made by Mother, my grandfather would go to the lounge for his forty winks. We were forbidden to wake him up, but things returned to normal when the muffin man, ringing his bell, roused him. This was a spectacle that has disappeared, just like the French onion men on their bicycles. The muffin man had a large tray on his head on which were the muffins, and we always bought them and toasted them in front of an open coal fire. Now the fireplaces have also disappeared.

When my Grandfather died, we inherited a small collection of Nigerian spears and decorated canoe paddles. Regrettably, over the years, these have decayed, their demise at times hastened by my brother and me 'playing' with them. Sadly they were consigned to the bonfire – and what a mistake that was! Mother did keep, for many more years, a long ivory anklet, which we sold in the 1980s. It was not a beautiful object, but perhaps we should have kept it in a cupboard.

My paternal grandfather was the seventh child of a blacksmith in the very small village of Great Orton in what is now Cumbria. Despite being physically of poor health as a child, on going to school at the age of eleven, he walked seven miles a day there and back and that presumably gave him the strength to join his cousins and friends in the local sport of Cumberland and Westmorland wrestling. He had some ability at this sport, in which strength and balance is vital, but he did not have the breadth of back which one of his nephews had, and it was this which helped the latter to win the Grasmere Middleweight Trophy three years running, and which he retained. From memory, this cup just about equalled the size of the FA Cup and my second cousin has it in the bank. Another sign of the times!

Grandpa Johnston left the north of England as a young man and came to London, where he eventually joined the Civil Service. He was a real character and for a man of such humble beginnings, he became a bit of a legend in his village. His working days included being the Secretary to Lord Chief Justice Stewart and the Clerk to the Official Arbitrator. For the work he did in the latter role he was awarded an Imperial Service Order, which is limited to 120 living persons. That is in one of my cupboards, but I find it difficult to believe that the next generation will keep such memorabilia.

As Father was away so much in the Second World War, my paternal grandfather was my aid and adviser for much of the time. He lived a few houses away from us, round the corner, and many years later my wife and I bought that same house, where our daughter and son were born. Brother Mick and I went one way to see grandparents, and so, years later, my kids went the other way to their grandparents. A very, very happy relationship at all times, and I frequently wonder why it is that so few families have such a harmonious existence.

My father also became a Civil Servant and when he left school the Headmaster said to my grandfather, 'Your son was not much good here, but he will do well in later life', and so he did. The first World War then intervened in his business life, and after being in the

Honourable Artillery Company, he joined the Royal Flying Corps and flew solo at Brooklands after only twenty minutes' instruction. He took off, then immediately knew that the wind would prevent him from turning. He side-slipped into the sewage farm, which ended his flying time but saved his life.

He was invalided out and then rejoined the services, where, together with a so-called uncle, he was posted to be a crew member in 'observation balloons'.

Father survived the war, ending his time in the mountains in Italy. Here he worked as an artillery observer, going up in a balloon tethered by hundreds of feet of cable high above the ground. He spotted for guns over enemy lines. Uncle was shot down, but his parachute opened and shut all the way down, luckily being open at the moment when he hit the ground, uninjured. Both Father and Uncle happily survived until well after World War II. Father was mentioned in dispatches, but it was only in 1998 that I found his certificate, signed by Winston Churchill.

Of sisters had I none, but my brother Howard (known then as Mick) arrived on the scene some three years after me in 1928 and my first memory of him is of one day in the garden of our house in Cheam, Surrey. At the time he was being a perishing nuisance. Because Mother was always insistent that I, being older, should not be too rough with him, I asked, 'What should I do?' She must have been watching the argument and said, 'If you do not hit him too hard, you may do it gently'. After some tears, peace was made.

Both grandfathers were sportsmen as were Father and Mother, and sports of all sorts have featured a great deal in my life so far. At school, I'm afraid to say that it took pride of place over learning work, and as in my father's case, post-school life had much more purpose than school days. I do not subscribe to the oft repeated phrase, 'the best days of your life are at school'.

Those days of the early 1930s seem long ago. Refrigerators were rare and we did not have one – a horse-drawn cart vending huge blocks of ice called every week and we put several large blocks in a big, lead-lined heavy wooden box which stood in our side entrance, and into which we put our bottles of milk and butter to keep them

Brother Mick and me, 1929.

fresh. The ice, of course, melted during the week and in the end that box too went on the bonfire and a refrigerator was purchased in its place.

All these descriptions of my relatives serve to show the type of genes that I inherited and that really *is* the lottery of life. What follows is, in essence, a reflection in many ways of the characteristics of my relatives. What happens subsequently is, to me, the mystery of life. What makes one turn left rather than right when decisions have to be made, and how does one know that by doing nothing, one might have done better than by changing course?

An early example to me of 'lateral thinking' arose on the occasions when Mother used to send me to my bedroom for being naughty. I pondered on how I might get on top of this punishment, so I used to lie on the bed and go to sleep. After a few such victories, my mother said, 'Go to your room and you are not to lie on the bed'. The answer I arrived at in my mind was to 'sit on the floor, wedge myself in one corner of the room, and go to sleep'. Mother came up, woke me up and I was not sent upstairs again! We often laughed about that. I have always been able to switch off and go to sleep even with other people around, and I was taught this when a Crusader on an outing in the country. Our leader told us to lie down in the field, think of nothing and sleep would follow, and it did.

Later in life, when I was at the second of my two merchant banks, I remembered all too vividly an episode of which I am not proud. We advertised for a vacancy to be filled in our investment management department, and when the applicant turned up for his interview, it was a very hot day. This did not help my state of mind, following a good luncheon with a tot or two (or was it three?) of wine. One very good trick when interviewing is to sit with the light behind you, leaving the interviewee facing into it. After the initial niceties of introduction, I asked him to tell me about himself and his background and why he thought he might fill the post. After only a few sentences from him, I knew he was not the right person but, to be kind to him, I let him prattle on. The sun behind my head got hotter and I am ashamed to say I dozed off – probably only for a few split seconds – but I came round suddenly and he was still talking. I did not change my mind; he did not get the job.

At kindergarten, Mother forbade the teachers to force me to write right-handed, because even then she knew that by switching left-handed kids into right-handed, it could make people stutter. Being left-handed is in fact an advantage because one is more ambidextrous than right-handed people. I can, for example, shoot equally well either way round – very useful in the Royal Marines much later on.

In those early days of the 1930s life seemed a very happy experience and as we had no car (until well after World War II), we bicycled everywhere. There was little chance of being knocked down by cars because there were not many around. When our next-door neighbour bought a shiny new baby Austin 7, everyone in the road turned out to have a look at it. As far as I can recall, that was the first car I ever saw. The Sports Club opposite our house in Cheam became one of the principal centres of my life and I joined in 1935 as a very junior tennis member – sixty-five years later I am still there. One of the very generous lady members who won Surrey Tennis Honours used to turn up on her horse when she was not playing. From this vantage point she would watch tennis and bowls – another thing unlikely ever to be seen again, certainly in our locality, where Meadowside Road is now probably twenty miles from a meadow. That generous lady, Leila Bennett, was the only member who ever turned up for tennis in a Rolls Royce.

We bicycled to school in Sutton three miles away. On the way home it was not unusual to get involved in contretemps with kids from other schools, which sometimes ended in minor fisticuffs – character-building I called it, but today it would probably be actionable in some court or other. Many of these 'enemies' became life-long friends, though for some, sadly, life was shortened by World War II. But for those of us who survived, conviviality has been solid and permanent.

One of my early prep school friends was Bob Schad, who played tennis at our club when we were some twelve years of age. Eventually he played hockey for England – how he survived to reach that very high level of success I will never know, because of an episode which I can even now vividly see and hear, and which was an unforgettable example of luck. Some four or five of us at our prep school were throwing quite large coloured rubber balls round in a square, when one of the others picked up a croquet ball, also coloured yellow, and threw that to Schad. With a loud clonk he headed it, and how he never complained or felt ill after such an impact I do not know. These accidents do happen, luckily not always serious, as we shall see from two other instances at a later stage, when I was at Epsom College.

From the middle 1930s I used to upset my father from time to time because I always came down early in the morning and while he was shaving, I used to grab the newspapers and read what I could before he took them from me; he then frequently had to straighten up all the pages. Reading papers has been a habit ever since, and because of my business career, the search for the *Financial Times* in later life, when on holidays, would frequently necessitate a walk of several miles – sometimes before breakfast, which was better than a pre-breakfast swim! Those readings of papers brought me face to face with war, and vivid recollections of two in particular are indelibly imprinted in my mind.: the Abyssinian War with the Italians, and the Spanish Civil War, and from then on right up to today, in the year 2001, this topic of war has seemingly hit the headlines virtually every day. What a price humanity pays for religious and political beliefs!

In the later 1930s – say from 1937 to 1938 – the fear of another world war intensified and affected one's thinking, even then at the age of thirteen, because things became progressively more serious. For the present generation, it may well be extremely difficult even to begin to contemplate life with very few cars, no television (which I did see first in 1938 at a school friend's house – and the set is still there), a half-mile walk to reach a bus service or perhaps a bicycle ride, often in rain or snow (it did snow in 1939-43 as we know) and a black-out with no street lights. The walk and bus ride to get to a cinema in wartime conditions, followed by the reverse journey to get back home again, took ages. Everything away from one's own home took so much longer than in today's age of the car, and conditions have reduced such simple journeys from, say, half an hour each way, to five minutes. But if traffic keeps growing, and perhaps if I live long enough, it seems possible that it will go back to one half hour each way again!

So far as I was concerned, in 1938, while I was still at preparatory school, two things came to the fore in my thinking. The first was passing the entrance examination into Epsom College, some three miles away by bicycle, and the second was the preparation for war, which appeared to be totally inevitable. As I mentioned earlier, school work was not my favoured subject – doing things was of far greater interest to me than learning, and homework was a punishment rather than a pleasure. Playing cricket and tennis were the first priority, and in fact, when I think about it, I am forced to conclude that cricket had something to do with me being alive in 1945 when the war ended, rather than possibly being dead, or worse still, severely injured. The reasons for this conclusion will be explained later. I do think that the lottery of life reaches its limits here, and decision-making takes over in directing which way one goes – for better or worse. One of my girl friends in the Sports Club, happily married to one of my oldest living friends, used to say to me on occasion: 'You are always so lucky'. After a few such statements over the years, I retorted one day that 'luck may occasionally be on one's side, but luck runs out in time,' and some of the apparent luck (or lack of it) has to result from one's choice of direction when problems of any sort have to be resolved.

In what used to be stock market vernacular, 'jobbing backwards' is a useless occupation, and when people have sometimes said to me in criticism, 'You are always so certain or blunt about things,' I have, sometimes retorted – wrongly, 'Yes, I know, but I cannot help it.' Vacillating is anathema to me and soon after joining the Royal Marines, I learned very quickly from the officers and non-commissioned officers, whom I hugely admired, that 'if you are asked a question, you give an answer.' This has been a benchmark in my attitude to office work and committee work ever since, and two particular examples of this will be revealed later, in interchanges first with the Headmaster of Epsom College, and second with the Chairman of Schroders, when I was at a critical stage of my City life.

CHAPTER TWO

The Run-Up to World War II

So, back to 1939, when my spare time at the age of fourteen was spent filling sandbags, helping in the building of the Air Raid Warden's posts, putting sticky paper in criss-cross patterns on all the windows of our house so that bombs would be prevented from showering people inside the house with glass fragments, and so on. While these simple tasks were undertaken by so many of us younger citizens, my mother, in common with thousands of other mothers, was making black-out curtains and talking about preparations for air raid shelters, keeping chickens and so on. What should have been the joyful time of one's life never happened, or, perhaps it would be better to say, it was truncated. This was the beginning of my education for real life (or death), and it helped to make me fatalistic about events and to take a rather serious view about life which has never left me.

My very dear wife, Cynthia, is only some five years younger than I and to a large extent, because of our background and early life experience, we have similar views on many things. We also have strong and differing views about politics and other matters as well, which makes for interesting evenings and sometimes heated discussions, but peace always reigns at the end of these debates, even if we beg to differ – and I do not always win. To my daughter Nicola and my son John, I can only apologize for these characteristically heated discussions, because we might have had more fun if I had been less emphatic. I trust, when they look back, that they will think that they did have fun, but both do take a serious view of life, and, through working hard, have been successful and happy in their own married lives. Maybe this is due to their genes, or have they been following an example? My choice is the former because, as we know, children do not always follow their parents in their attitudes and behaviour.

In August 1939, for the third time in four years, we went on holiday to Southwold in Suffolk and, as was normal, Father had his usual almost daily 'black bag' (or was it red?) of papers from the Court of Protection for his perusal and blessing or otherwise. One day amongst those papers came a clear sign that the balloon might go up. We left for home a few days early, and the day war broke out is as clear to me now as it was then. It was a beautiful sunny day and the grass courts opposite our house were full of tennis players enjoying the game. We sat in the lounge and I can still see my father, tense and serious, as we listened to Prime Minister Chamberlain saying over the radio that 'we must consider ourselves at war with Germany.' About two – or was it three – minutes after he had finished, the air raid sirens sounded and within a flash the courts were deserted. It was the first time we had heard these, otherwise than as a practice, but it was a false alarm. Some of those players never appeared again, I am sorry to say.

Father then had the responsibility of evacuating a fair portion of the Civil Service to Cambridge, and for five years his office was situated in the new buildings of Caius College, facing the market square. He came home every second or third Friday for the weekend and Mother in effect looked after my brother and me. In Mick's case this continued for the whole of the war, but not in mine. On the 3rd September 1943 I joined the Royal Marines. Before that, however, I had left my Preparatory School in Sutton and, by the skin of my teeth, had passed the entrance examination to Epsom College, having taken part of the examination a second time. It was at about this time that my father told me something that even now I find it hard to believe. He had been Chief Clerk to the House of Lords – or was it the Commons? Whichever it was, I know where his office was because I had been there and can see it now. He must have felt stuck at some stage of his time there, because, of all things, he visited a fortune teller who, out of the blue, said to him, 'You have two sons and for their good you will have to move your job.' I find this so out of context that I still cannot believe it, but he did just that, and in so doing took a minute cut in salary. The purpose of recording this is that for my brother and me this move opened the door to life in the

City of London and the financial world, in my case starting in 1941, when I left Epsom College. Mick left in 1944 and started his life in the City in the same firm.

Before that, however, in my life a two-year interval has to be allowed for. I bicycled to Epsom College every day of those two years, bar of course school holidays, and for those two years I thank my father and mother for their struggle to pay the school fees as a day boy (£30 a term for each of two of us). It took a sizeable portion of Father's salary, which was around £900 a year, and I think my memory, always good for figures, is not far out. In real terms, in today's money, this must be about £90,000 a year because £1 of those days is close to one penny in today's currency.

In those two years, I seemed to be bottom but one in my form every term (bottom of all was Pat Rafferty, who became managing director of his business and a successful RNVR pilot). As usual, however, I did very well at sports. At cricket my highest score was 144, and at shooting (.22) I was in the College VIII – a great asset to me later in both these sports. In that innings of 144 I broke three cricket bats, one mine, one a fellow student's (who was not amused) and one the College's, but I do not think my parents paid for the latter two. Two events in the field of athletics occurred right in front of me and would surely hit the headlines in today's highly regulated conditions. One was when throwing the discus around a large circle with four of us practising to spin our bodies and let go of the heavy disc correctly. I threw mine in the direction of the luckless Rafferty aforementioned, who had turned his back on me to pick up the previous one. The one aimed in his direction scored a bull's eye on his fair-sized stern end at the base of his spine. All he did was turn round and say, 'You fool.' My reply was 'You should watch the ball.' The second incident, with an even worse possible outcome, occurred when the boy in front of me threw a javelin which veered to the left. Instead of running away, one of the spectators ducked. It landed with quite a crunch on the back of his skull behind his right ear and actually penetrated it. To everyone's astonishment he stood there, held the javelin, and someone else pulled it out. He lived to tell the story but how he did I do not know. That really was the luck of the devil. One would think that athletics might be considered a safe sport, but accidents happen all the time, and just for once I have to say that I fully approve of all the rules and regulations constructed to try to stop such incidents.

Epsom College, originally started as the Royal Medical Foundation, is a very fine public school where sons of doctors are admitted at cheaper fee rates, and there are many scholarships for them to aim at. Therefore leavers entering the medical profession used to account for over half of departing sixth formers. My first head of house (a day-boy house) was Alan Parks, who later became President of the Royal College of Surgeons and was knighted. He exercised, as Head Boy of Epsom, a rarely used privilege whilst at the College of having a dog with him all the time. I know because as a new boy I was his 'fag' for a while and it was often in his 'bin'. He used to say that the only other privilege for the Head Boy was that he could be married, but I am sure that has never been permitted.

Whilst at the College I was bottom of my Mathematics form and was sent for by the master concerned, who said he wanted to demote me to a lower level class. My immediate reply was, 'Sir, someone has to be bottom and I will learn more from you than I will from Mr Weir' – I stayed. An early lesson in tact, I felt: flattery does sometimes get you somewhere.

Two particularly good friends at that time were Derek Scheerboom, later to become Medical Officer for Health in Epsom and Ewell, and Basil Smith, who left to join the Royal Air Force. The latter became a bomber pilot and after a raid in Germany when another plane crashed on landing back at base, his Commanding Officer asked for a volunteer to take its crew for a ride around to help settle their nerves. Tragically, in low cloud or fog, Basil's plane hit a hillside and all were killed – the first wartime death of a close friend. I wrote a letter to his mother, did not really know what to say, and threw it in the waste paper basket. I am ashamed about this, but being new to such events, chickened out, which I have not done since and hope never to do again. Sadly, when one reaches a certain stage in life's span, one gets rather used to this agonizing duty.

Others to join up included R.H. (Dick) Kendall, also a house prefect, who joined the Royal Navy. One Saturday at our local church I asked him what he was doing. Nothing much, he said, and two weeks' later he earned a Distinguished Service Order for the midget submarine raid on the German battleship Tirpitz. He is still alive and I corresponded with him in Canada only recently, in late 1998. At the College I saw a well-dressed, smart Royal Marine who was on leave named Russell Reynolds, and thought he was huge. Some thirty years later at an Old Epsomian dinner, sitting opposite a chap called Reynolds who was well short of my height, I said I only knew of a *Russell* Reynolds who had joined the Marines and had played in the band on HMS *Dorsetshire*, which was sunk by the Japanese in the Indian Ocean. He said, 'How the hell do you remember that?' and I replied somewhat to the effect that I had been in the Marines as well and that his swimming activities had remained in my mind.

Trying to study in the evenings after a long day at school (hours 08.15 chapel, games all afternoon, lessons again at 4-ish and then compulsory prep in the House Common Room) and getting home frequently as air raids began at 7pm – these, as I have said before, were not factors that motivated me towards the academic side of life. My brother and I had had an offer to go to America to escape whatever might have befallen us by staying, but we declined – correctly in my view. Evenings at home were often spent under the kitchen table or, on some nights, under the staircase in the hall cupboard – not much room for Mother, brother and me, but we survived at the expense of learning, and the culmination of all this was to come in September 1941 when Father, who I knew was struggling financially, asked me whether I would like to join a Merchant Bank in the City. I had not the slightest idea what that might be but said 'yes'. The introduction to Helbert, Wagg & Co Ltd – later to become Schroders – came about following upon the episode mentioned earlier about Father and the Fortune Teller. Because he moved to the Court of Protection, he did in fact do us a good turn in two strangely coincidental events (another lottery prize?).

One of his bosses was a bachelor named Frank Ratto, who took an interest in my brother and me, and one of Ratto's friends was Alfred Wagg, Chairman of Helbert, Wagg and a fellow member of the Garrick Club. Early in the month of September 1941, I went to the City with my father who left me at 41 Threadneedle Street while he went on to Cambridge. I had a couple of hours' interview and a sort of mathematics paper to answer, which I did not complete correctly, I remember, but got the job of being a very junior clerk in a prestigious and well-known small merchant bank. On receiving a letter offering me the post at a salary of £65 a year (Say £6,000 today), and not knowing what was going to happen in the war or with my parents' bank balances, I discussed it with Father on one of his home weekends and said I would take it. He said if I did get the job, I would never get to the top because I was not born in the right bed or had not gone to the right school. (He was of course referring to Eton, which bred so many City bowler hats). His statement was a challenge in itself, and although then possibly true, it would not be so now, as the competition is open to all and the hours of work are so horrendous. It is now more likely to be the case of the best man or woman who wins, rather than being the son of whomsoever, who gets the promotion.

Then came my first real left- or right-turn decision. I went to see the Headmaster of Epsom College four days after term began in October 1941 and said, 'Sir, I am leaving.' He replied, 'When?' I said, 'Now.' There was a pregnant silence because he knew, as did I, that I had only passed what today would be three 'O' levels, one being mathematics, the second English language and the third English literature, the last being a paper on *Hamlet* which, by a complete accident, I had done three years' running. After a pause he said, 'Are you sure about this?' I replied, 'Yes' His response was 'This is the biggest mistake you will ever make in your life.' I replied, 'We shall have to see about that.' As I rode my aforementioned bicycle out of the College gates, I reminded myself what Churchill had achieved with no examinations and said to myself, 'I will damn well drive my Bentley through these gates before I die, to prove him wrong.' Whether the result has been achieved or not in the exact meaning of that statement I am not sure – I do not have a Bentley but a Lexus will do! – a Bentley seems a bit too upmarket to me and there are better things that one can do with money.

To some extent that finished my formal education, but life itself has done the rest. After the war I did three years of evening classes for three nights a week at The City of London College to prepare for the Chartered Institute of Secretaries examinations. When asked by the tutor when I was taking the examination, I replied that I was not, and he just about exploded. That is the only time when a teacher has had the cheek and stupidity to say to me that 'learning' was a waste of time. The reason I could not take the examination was because, in spite of being commissioned in the Royal Marines, I would have had to go back to 'school' and take the requisite 'O' level examinations. Because of the pressure of work, I could not possibly find the time and I am not sure that it would have made any difference even if I had done so. I rather feel that a different course of life would have ensued, which would, in all probability, have been rather dull.

Returning to early City days, I had two years of commuting before joining up and I really had to start at the bottom. From having a pre-war staff of 100 or so, they were down to thirteen. I was No 13 (my lucky number) and I really did sit on a high stool before a huge ledger, at which I had to learn 'columnar book keeping.' Adding machines were heavy and clumsy and took ages to use, so by sheer necessity I learned that I could add up two columns of figures at once and beat someone on a machine. Everything was done long-hand, and when the dividends on our investment trust companies had to be paid, the huge sheets of calculations had four years of lateral space to cover four dividend payments per shareholder. Faced with all that, I really did discover what colour blindness did for me. From time to time I had to ask which colour of figures we were in – at least traffic lights internationally are the same way up!

It was during these two years that I joined the Home Guard ('Dad's Army') and we really did do arms drill with sticks. Epsom College had rifles that worked. To join, I put two years on my age and no one questioned it, and it was during evening training sessions that we learned judo or unarmed combat: how, for example, to throw a 15-stone man over your back when you only weighed nine stone, how to take a rifle off a man who faced you, or how to knock out a man who had a pistol at your back. All very useful training for what came later in 1943.

The strange thing to me is that I remember very little of those early wartime days in the City. I suppose we accepted as a way of life having to go down to the bank cellars during air raids, but it was an experience. I had some excellent, much older, male colleagues who tried to teach me a little, some of which has stuck firmly in my mind. One colleague was a remarkable dealer named George Wood who, in his time, was a City legend – it was said that he had made a million pounds before the war in foreign bonds, and then lost it during the war – not a surprise – but it was also said, and I believe it, that he made it back again before he died. Much of this was the firm's but some was certainly on his own account. On one post-war meeting I asked him some question about gilt-edged securities or some such 'paper' investment, and he jumped at me and said forcibly, 'Young man, there is only one thing you do with paper and that is not dealing in it.' I leave you to imagine what he meant, but coupled with my first post-war boss, Michael Verey, these two were 'equity'-minded people. I have never personally invested in fixed interest securities for my family, myself or clients, if they would let me, but much more of that in later chapters on investment and money generally.

In those days, and particularly in those nights, the bombing of London came and to some extent went, but oddly enough I have no recollection of trains running late very often. The nearest thing to real trouble for me was on occasion when we were coming towards a tunnel. We heard bullets or cartridges which landed on the carriage roof from a plane flying above us, but when we emerged from the tunnel, all was normal, thank heavens. In a cricket match one weekend, when the London docks were heavily bombed and planes seemed to be all too close, we did all run into a ditch and stayed there for a while before going back to the game – who won was irrelevant. It was during those two years before joining the Royal Marines that my father, who, as will be recalled, was in the Royal Flying Corps, was asked by a neighbour, Squadron Leader Denis Francis, if they could have a few words and a short walk. Denis was a regular RAF

Shoreham Aerodrome, 1915. Father in rear seat of plane.

Officer and he flew, amongst other planes, experimental bombers which had large rings attached below them and which were used to fly low over the sea when the electric charge in the ring would blow up electronic mines – known as de-gauzing. Leaning over a farm gate, Denis said to Father, 'You flew in World War I and will understand what I am going to say – I will not return from my next flight and I have to tell someone who will understand.' He did not return, and was lost somewhere in the English Channel. I have often wondered how many such stories are true, but perhaps, more to the point, how many did return and the forecasts of death just got forgotten.

Knowing that I was colour blind, I knew that entry into the Royal Navy was not really likely to succeed, but I also knew that the Royal Marines were (then) largely a sea-going force (not nowadays), and I have always liked discipline, order, fitness and, I suppose, being somewhat different. Therefore, on the back of my school Cadet Force learning and experience in Dad's Army, I volunteered early in 1943 and was ordered to attend an interview in Queen Anne's Mansions in the West End of London. The chairman of the interview

THE RUN-UP TO WORLD WAR II

My matchstick warships, 1944: HMS Coventry, *HMS* Dorsetshire, *HMS* Kempenfelt, *HMS* Hood *unfinished, all on the same scale.*

board was Captain Sherbrooke VC, who had a black patch over one eye, the result of convoy action when on HMS *Onslow*. After the preliminary questions, such as 'Why do you wish to volunteer for the Royal Marines?', he said, 'You have an unusual hobby – tell us about it.' I showed him photographs, and then referred to my many hundreds of hours of making model Royal Navy ships out of matchsticks from plans adapted to scale from *Jane's Fighting Ships*. Some 10,000 matchsticks had been stuck together with seccatine and shaped with razor blades and sandpaper. The rigging was cotton; the guns and torpedo tubes all revolved. He then said, 'Come over here and tell me what these are.' He pointed to a table full of lead model warships, and as far as I know, I got all the names correct. After a period of probably only a minute or so (it seemed like ages), I was called back into the interview room, faced the board and was told I was 'in'. 'Order papers will follow at the appropriate time'. This was the first time I proved to some extent that 'bullshit baffles brains,' and this time it worked. The ships are now in the loft and they really do look as though they have been through a battle. The masts have been broken by things falling on to them or by birds flying around up there which have been seeking a way out, or else the glue has weakened. They will need many hours of dockyard refit to bring them back to life, but I guess that in the end they really will land up on the bonfire. Incidentally, I have just recalled that in a fund-raising for the Royal Navy week in the City of London, I took them up to a shop window in Lombard Street, where they just might have helped cash to flow.

CHAPTER THREE

The Royal Marines

ON 3RD SEPTEMBER 1943, I reported to Lympstone in Devon with many others. We were marched from Topsham station to what is now the Royal Marines Commando Training Centre and, still in our 'civvies', were halted before a very fine wooden hut (it is still there and does bring back memories). On falling out to find our huts, one of us, a Geordie, shouted at a portly figure leaning on the balcony rails, 'Hey, Tubbie, where do we get the eats?' He had shouted at a Company Sergeant Major!

One of our instructors, Corporal Stewart, asked us where we all lived. I said, 'Cheam, Corporal'. He lived in the next village, Ewell, and his family were long-standing friends of my eventual in-laws. Sadly, he died some years after but by another odd twist, his widow married a second time to a widower in our Sports Club, John Worthington. Both play excellent bowls and when he was ninety years of age, I had the pleasure of taking him to the REME Headquarters near Reading. It was in World War II that John had ended his active service as a Lt. Colonel in REME. REME and the Royal Marines are very closely connected, as we shall see later. I have been, again by coincidence, an honorary adviser to both of the Museums of these fine Corps.

In our squad were several policemen, who did their best to tell us innocent youngsters all about the facts of life. Where most are now I know not, but I kept in touch, on and off, with three non-policemen. One was Philip Bates, son of the family which 'was' Cunard. Another was (?) Crick, whose father was Chaplain of the Fleet, and the third was Alastair Walker. All of them are mentioned later. Thus began three very happy, formative and thoroughly worthwhile years, and apart from my family, the Corps has featured largely in my life ever since, as have my Sports Club, the City and the charity world. It really was a correct decision to have made. I had volunteered at seventeen and a half for the Marines, rather than waiting for an initial draft into whatever service or regiment came out of the hat.

For the first two or three weeks we were not allowed out of barracks (known in the Royal Marines as 'going ashore') and our first such liberty was nearly a disaster. It is difficult in today's conditions to believe that at the age of eighteen most of us did not drink, although smoking was commonplace. Father had given me a cigarette case and a pipe and tobacco pouch at sixteen. Now some of us – and I was one – drank scrumpy for the first time. It was a hot sunny day and the effect was a shock to the system – scrumpy is rough cider and very alcoholic, How we got back to camp without being caught or reprimanded I do not know. A good example of 'undiscovered crime' and I have never drunk cider since. Pay for recruits was incredibly low, even for those days, and every Friday we were lined up in turns, stood to attention in front of the desk in the Pay Office, and answered, 'Yes, Sir' to our names. We were then handed the princely sum of £1.50 in cash. Some of us who worked in the City of London were exceedingly fortunate because our companies made up our service pay to that which we had been earning up to call-up day. I have the records of this generous and extraordinary gesture, which, until I was commissioned, in effect doubled my service pay. This was fairly unique and must have cost the shareholders of Helbert Wagg quite a large sum of money, but it was hugely appreciated by all of us.

This generosity did not lift my total earnings for the next year to a sum sufficient to go ashore and have a full-blown dinner out, but a fellow recruit, Alastair Walker, became a very good friend. Every Saturday of those first three months when we were together, he would say, 'We are going to Exmouth to the Imperial Hotel for dinner.' On the first occasion I replied that there was no way I could afford such an outing (and in any case I had never been to an hotel for dinner), but he said, 'I just want your company and I have enough income to pay for it, so we are going.' We did just that for several weeks, and the luxury of each outing included a bath in hot water and clean warm towels before eating. What the officer guests thought of us being in their company I can only guess, because in those days the gap between officers and men was considerable (thank goodness it is so much narrower today), but we were always on our best behaviour just in case.

When watching many of today's television programmes about military training, we all too often see Non-Commissioned Officers, and indeed on occasions, Commissioned Officers, shouting at their men and swearing at them. I now know that when such films, which in a sense are meant to be documentaries, are made, the producers cannot be controlled in what they produce. That I believe is a scandal because they often give quite the wrong impression. I can obviously only speak from my own experience, but I cannot recall any instructor swearing at us or using foul language. Certainly, and quite correctly, they cajoled us and pushed us hard, especially in our Officer Cadet Training Unit (OCTU), where, physically and mentally, we were driven as hard as possible to see who could or could not stand the pressure. At such stages it was quite common to see Corporals and Sergeants carrying the rifle of a cadet in order to help him through the course, providing of course the chap was not 'swinging the lead'. This phrase, for those who were not in the naval services, referred to sailing days when a lucky man swung the line from the side of a ship to see how deep the lead weight went before it hit the bottom. I think some recent ship tragedies in the Mediterranean might not have happened if there had been a linesman on watch!

After some six weeks at Lympstone, we were marched up to Exmoor (Dalditch Camp) for a further six weeks or so of fairly tough training in what was a bitterly cold winter. We did have literally to break the ice some mornings to shave, but it was here that I learned another lesson in life. One of the new Marines, older than I, stood next to me by a notice board and asked what the notices meant. I did not realize at the time, but I later understood that he could not read. I am sometimes accused of being blunt and lacking consideration, but on this occasion, for some odd reason, I did not even remotely try to 'take the mickey'. I explained what were the orders and never thought any more about it until a week or so later, when he went AWOL (absent without leave). However, he only went after pinching something from almost everyone in the hut – except me, and I think that was his way of saying 'thank you'. Although I can be blunt on occasions, or as my friends might well say, 'definite', I cannot recall ever belittling someone less fortunate than I have been and I trust I never will. It was at my spell at Lympstone that I collected my one and only 'extra parade'. A Sunday church service and parade in bright sunlight was the day when, being 'tallest on the left', the Sergeant Major walked round me eyeing me up and down. Then he came back, stood in front of me and asked, 'Did you shave this morning?' I was somewhat taken aback and retorted, 'Yes, Sergeant Major I did and I can prove it.' He replied, 'Stand closer next time – extra parade.' I then suffered the punishment of running twice round the enormous parade ground overlooking the River Exe with my rifle held above my head with arms fully extended. The Major who officiated asked me how, being a 'Y Scheme entrant' (we had a badge showing we might be officer material), I had erred. He laughed at my answer, administered the punishment and said, 'Do not do it again.' I often used to think of this when putting a new blade in my razor, but nowadays one gets a new razor and throws away the old one. The next posting was to Deal for the pre-OCTU, where physical fitness was pushed hard with long cross-country schemes in limited time, carrying some sixty or more pounds weight in one form or another ('yomping', I suppose in today's terminology). The longest such effort was one of over forty miles in fifteen hours! It was after one spell of this, lasting some weeks, that I came home on leave and slept 24 hours – what a waste of a day!

While at Deal on one of these schemes, we rounded a hill at some 200 feet above sea level and at that level saw dozens of anti-aircraft guns in a long line, well spaced out and following the contour line.

This was an unusual sight to say the least, and we all wondered what on earth was going to happen, being almost as near to France as one could be. We did not have long to wait for the answer, because a night or two later those in bed were woken up by a new and strange noise. I was on guard duty, patrolling the barracks grounds, and that noise, combined with the anti-aircraft gunfire, was almost deafening. The next day, the papers printed 'Pilotless planes bomb London' – or words to that effect; we had heard and seen the first Doodle Bugs (V.1's), which really did make one's hearts speed up after the engines cut out – where were they going to land? We did then begin to wonder how long the war would last.

Presumably because of the result of enquiries following an accident in Freshwater Bay, Wales, in April 1943, when two landing craft sank with the loss of thirty-nine Royal Marines and six Royal Naval personnel, Alastair Walker and I were withdrawn from our course and sent to Stonehouse Barracks, Plymouth to await further instructions. Our removal was on the grounds of colour-blindness. It is believed that the vessels had collided due to crews not knowing green from red navigation lights, but I have never been able to confirm this. Walker's father knew the then Commandant General, Royal Marines, and, to cut the story short, we were sent for by the Brigade Major, Major Pym. 'How the hell can you chaps appeal to the CG?' he said, 'There is a war on you know.' We stated that we had both signed forms as 'Y' Scheme entrants, that if we passed all expected tests, physical and mental, we would receive our commissions, and that because of this accident, the rules had been changed. His reply was, 'You can transfer to the army tomorrow with an automatic commission, or return to the RMOCTU. If you pass, you will go into the Commandos, but never to sea.' We replied that we would go back and hopefully pass, but that the restrictions were back to front. If I was a Commanding Officer of a ship, or on watch on the bridge, I would always see that I had a man with me who was *not* colour-blind, and therefore knew which way we were going. If, however, in the Commandos, I might well be the only person with my head over the parapet when the coloured Verey light was fired. If I got the colour wrong, I might well go the wrong way with the possibility of either getting shot for cowardice or getting the VC for being the opposite.

I have often wondered what accidents colour-blind people cause. How, for instance, does a colour-blind doctor know if you have a sore throat and what about a chemist or scientist with coloured pills or powders, or an electrician with coloured wires? I am sure he will not mind my telling this, but many years after the war I was lunching at

Portsmouth when I learned from his wife that General Sir Peter Whiteley was colour-blind. He had naval wings on his uniform and how, I wonder, did he know which way the ship was going when trying to land on an aircraft carrier at night? Possibly the wash would tell such a pilot.

This is an aside, so back to training in cold weather. One example of this was a map-reading exercise on foot from Thurlstone to Okehampton and back, done mostly at night and in threes. It froze hard and snowed equally hard, and, when in the middle of nowhere, we were completely lost. We were joined by three others, thus making six of us, and with the aid of an RAF escape compass which my father had given me, we completed the five-day course. The oil in our prismatic compasses had frozen and none of the other thirty chaps completed the test. The next weekend those thirty men had to do that section again whilst we six stayed in Thurlstone Hotel, which we had to ourselves. The CO said, 'No-one would get his commission if he could not read a map or use a compass.' Many years later, a retired colonel came to dinner at our home in Ewell. He turned up late by over half an hour because he lost the way from Putney and went as far as Guildford before he realized his error – only some twenty miles further each way!

In the end both Walker and I received our commissions and when I passed out at Thurlstone, the ceremony, witnessed by no one, took place in a field near the church. It was bitterly cold and it had snowed hard the night before. When we were dismissed, we turned to the right, as was usual on such an order, counted to three and then fell out. Why that was the routine, and still is, I do not know, but one man stood fast. It was (now) Second Lieutenant Richard Bradley RM, and he was still at attention, sloping arms. It was the last time we were to hold rifles and he was unconscious on his feet; we carried him off still vertical.

My promotion had been held up through being burnt with phosphorous. This delayed things a month or so, but it proved to be a winning lottery ticket because some of my earlier course members were killed, whereas I went to India, where the war ended following upon the explosion of the atomic bombs in Japan. That event saved

Father, Lieutenant, Royal Flying Corps, 1916.

Father and me, 1945. I am wearing the same Sam Browne!

hundreds of thousands of Allied personnel and other lives, and I have never understood those who campaigned for 'ban the bomb'. It was the best thing that ever happened. They started that phase of the war, not us.

My last social occasion in India was meeting afresh Marine Crick, and he suggested that we might have dinner in Bombay. This we did, and he knew that he would have to pay the bill because I had no more rupees left – I am sure that was against the rules. If he reads this, I trust he will give me a call, because I would love to repay the gesture with far better wine than we had in 1946.

After the war I met one of my three other room mates, Lt. Tony Jary, several times in the City over the following three years or so, because he worked in the nearby building of The British Linen Bank. Many years after that I asked him if he would join the RM Officers' Dinner Club, because he would have known several of 48 Commando, Royal Marines, and he said he would. I wondered for a while why he had not. Then I had a mighty shock which brought a lump to my throat when I saw a bench with his name on it in the memorial garden of the Royal Marines Museum in Eastney.

One last story about Major Pym (I do not think he recognized me) has always amused me. On being commissioned, I was, quite extraordinarily, posted by him to the selfsame company in Plymouth which I had left to return to the OCTU, so I knew some of the chaps with whom I had lived in the same barrack rooms. They could not pull the wool over my eyes. I played cricket quite well, as I have said before, and one morning the Commandant, Col. Webb Bowen, said, 'You are playing cricket tomorrow, Johnston.' I said I was Duty Officer and he repeated, 'You are playing cricket tomorrow, Johnston' – so I obeyed. We played against the Royal Australian Air Force Sunderland Flying Boat Reconnaissance Squadron. Trevor Bailey of England and Essex fame (also an RM Officer) was on our side and whether we won or lost I know not, but I will guess we won! The Aussies asked me to have a day flying with them, which I jumped at, and when I asked Major Pym for a day off from RM duties, he said, 'Good God, you might get killed. You had better sign this form so that if you are, we take no responsibility for your action.' It was a great experience, and by another odd chance I flew to Karachi, India, to join the Amphibious Support Regiment RM in a Sunderland Flying Boat with only some dozen passengers. That was a splendid, slow and very comfortable way to travel – bags of room, armchairs which were not fixed to the deck, and flights of only a few hours at a time, calling at Marseilles, Sicily, Cairo (landing on the Nile), Lake Habbanya, Bahrain and then Karachi. The flying time lasted thirty-two and a half hours and took four days! The three young Royal Marine Officers on the flight had never been beyond Plymouth, and when we took off from Poole Harbour, I thought of my father's talk with Squadron Leader Denis Francis. When Blighty disappeared in the misty sunlight, I too wondered if I would ever see it again.

In India the posting to the Amphibious Regiment was more than interesting. I had never seen a tank close to, let alone been on one, and at midnight on the day of arrival at Mahd Island, north of Bombay, the Commanding Officer, Colonel Wills RM, said I would be in charge of the Supply Train on the assault on Singapore, so I had better go and see one and have a day or two of indoctrination. In the event it lasted one day, because I got nearer to death that day than I have ever been before or since. These huge American amphibious tanks were track-propelled on land, while at sea they had a 900-horsepower engine in them and the basic model had a ramp door at the back of a large empty well deck. The unit, from memory, had a squadron of basic models for supply and transportation roles, a squadron of models where the well deck was filled by flame-throwers, and another squadron with guns in the well deck. After a quick run along the shore and up and down sand dunes, where you cannot see what is in front of you as you go over the top (hair-raising, to put it bluntly), we then went out to sea, where the monsoon winds were still blowing. I was told to sit on the top with my feet in front of me just about in the sea, and to hang on for dear life to the only bollard to my right. That was the understatement of the year; I had to do just that. Huge waves came at me and I had been told of men being swept off and killed by hitting the ramp doors at the back. I did not let go, but the strain of hanging on tore some tendons in my right arm so that it was effectively paralysed the next morning when I

Father and Mother, 1945.

woke up. That ended my war, but the war also ended a few weeks afterwards in any case – my several months' stay in India consisted of staying in a flat with two other naval personnel overlooking the seafront in Bombay, and after daily treatment by an RN physiotherapist for many weeks every morning, I spent the afternoons in the Bombay Cricket Club playing billiards, swimming and reading up economics and mathematics. This was because I knew my job was being held open for me. 'How did you win the war, daddy?' I hear.

One last story about Bombay. One evening when we had just received our 'booze' rations, the four of us in our 'cabin' were playing liar dice, and some time near midnight the spots on the dice were getting somewhat blurred. Bad lighting! A noisy couple in the street were bawling at the tops of their voices, and one of us went to the balcony and shouted to them to 'Stop it' – or something stronger! The response was, 'Do you want a fight?' We said, 'Yes, come up!' They did. Alas, suffering from an excess of alcohol, we discovered very quickly that our invitees were Denis Compton of cricket fame and Peter Judge of Essex County. We had a good laugh, followed by a good night, and in a temperature of well over 90°, saw Compton hit a hundred next day in the Bombay Cricket Ground.

For some weeks I used to go into the nets with the Indian Test Team and spent many hours bowling to them. Being left-handed, I was able to do this, but batting was not really on because two-handed activities were at that stage not possible – luckily that has corrected itself over the years.

The return to England was on the Merchant Liner *Georgic* and she was filled with the largest draft of naval personnel. Freddie Mills of boxing fame gave demonstrations every day on the forecastle, and some two to three weeks later we landed back at Liverpool in a snow storm.

PART II

A Career in Merchant Banking

Chapter One

Back to Merchant Banking: Helbert Wagg/Schroder Wagg

WE WERE DEMOBILIZED in the April of 1946 and before returning to civvy street (to Helbert Wagg & Co Ltd), we all had, as a preliminary, to receive our demob clothes. This was a bit of a pantomime but as none of us had civvy clothes, we had to wear what we drew for some time ensuing. Mine went the way of all things as soon as possible, but I did wear the trilby hat for a few months – all men wore them then, as one frequently sees in post-war films. Mine left my head vertically in a gust of wind in the middle of London Bridge, but following my military training, I marched steadily onwards, pretending that it was not mine but following it with one eye as it descended on to the road to be run over by both the off-side wheels of a double-decker bus. I have never worn a hat to work since.

On return to Threadneedle Street, I was interviewed by the Manager, 'Copper' Barnes, a DCM and MM from World War I who was commissioned in the Field. He was a Major in World War II and was not a man whom you saw after lunchtime if you could help it. In those days, City lunches for the bosses were lengthy affairs, where pre-lunch drinks and port afterwards helped many to be less tolerant in the afternoons – so I saw him in the morning. He asked what I wanted to do and although I had no idea, I said I would like to start on the first floor, where I knew managers had their rooms. 'Chaps who have joined fine regiments should be rewarded,' he said, so he fixed it. Across the City, starting salaries were around £200 a year, which was the standard salary for returned ex-servicemen, whatever rank they had been. He did me a good turn that day, and turning left – or was it right? – was the correct request.

My immediate boss then was Michael Butcher, who had been in the Hampshire Regiment. He had been captured by the Germans at

Green Hill in North Africa and spent several years as a prisoner of war. He was so used to sleeping every afternoon that nearly every day in the office for many months he did just that. I know because he sat opposite me. The only other colleague in that room was Jimmy Langley, who was bi-lingual in French. He had been captured in France, having had most of one arm blown off. He escaped back to England and was involved in what I now assume was SOE (Special Operations Executive) work until the war ended. He finished the war as a Lieutenant Colonel. Typical of the man was a picture he showed us of him in a queue in Paris with German soldiers each side of him. He really did look French with his beret firmly on his head. He had a mechanical hand fitted, and on his return from Roehampton Hospital one afternoon, he came into the room, took it off, threw it on the desk and said, 'There you are, something you buggers cannot do.' In the next room was our Director, James O'Brien (MC from World War I) and when he came in from time to time to see Mike Butcher, he used to say, 'Tell him to pop in when he wakes up.' I cannot see anyone being so tolerant today. It is amazing to me how the hours of work have changed since those days in 1946. Our expected time to start work was 9.45 am and the time to go home was 5.00 pm, and we had one hour for lunch – a total expected work time of six and a quarter hours per day, or thirty-one hours a week, but in merchant banking you are expected to work either in the office or at home to keep up to date. No overtime was paid for this, but if you sought promotion, you simply had to do what was necessary. Today many City people are in their office by 8.00 am and certainly do not finish much before 6.00 pm – lunch is more often than not a sandwich at one's desk, so work time can be some ten hours per day or fifty hours a week. Certainly the pay is proportionately much higher, but job security hardly exists in many cases. Coupled with all the well-known strain on home and family life, I know which I would rather have, and at least most of those of my generation who stayed the course have pensions, which are as certain as anything can be these days.

And so began a very happy and instructive spell of many years working for a private merchant bank where the directors were much older men. The thought of ever becoming a Manager of a Department before reaching the age of fifty was quite ridiculous. Progress in those days was very slow, but so was life generally, and there was time for a bit of fun.

Very early on Butcher said to me that the best way to start climbing the ladder was to find something in which to specialize, and I can remember all too clearly thinking to myself that that would prove difficult: surely there was nothing on the horizon that had not been done already by someone else. *That* target really came into sight some five or more years later. Our Chairman was Alfred Wagg, a very kindly man, who lived in East Grinstead and was looked after by his chauffeur, Townsend. My first encounter with Alfred Wagg was during the two years before joining the Royal Marines. While standing by his desk at that time, he gave me a pair of scissors and asked me to trim his jacket cuffs. He was not using clothes coupons on new suits, and he regarded this attitude as part of his war effort. When we returned to the City in 1946, he began to ask the young men to have luncheon with him in the Directors' dining room, so long as there were no VIPs present. That was a privilege, and he used to pull our legs pretty hard. On one of these occasions he told me to carve the goose; I had never seen one, let alone carved one, and did not know which end to begin. He had a beautiful house in East Grinstead with large grounds and at times he would ask four of us to go down for the weekend to play tennis and croquet with him. A lasting story he told us made me realize that it is not always what you know but who you know that matters. He had a brand new Humber Super Snipe, which was an unusual sight on the road because new cars were then like gold dust. He said he had waited so long for one that he had written to Lord Rootes saying that if he had to wait much longer, would he please deliver it to the next world! He got it in a week. When he died, he left a sum of money to each member of the staff, numbering then over 100, and his house and grounds went to the local Nurses' Charity.

Another director, Albert Palache, was reputed never to have had a dirty pound note in his hand. When my brother was counting out £50 worth of white fivers, he got to number nine. At that point

Palache banged his hand on the counter and said, 'Never count the last one – there might be two.' I still follow that tip. Palache once stopped an older colleague of mine on the staircase and said, 'We have not met before have we?' Answer, 'I have been here over fifteen years, Sir, but away in the war.' He lived in another world, but all the Board then were gentlemen in every sense of the word – there was time for a little grace and 'thankyous' were more frequent than of late. There is no complaint about this – it is the way things have developed, but as I said earlier, pay rises were also small. These averaged no more than £75 per year for ten years, and my target for a salary of £1,000 by the age of thirty was just missed, but we did get bonuses in those days, sometimes of over £300, which helped. Thank heavens the uncertainty of this ended in 1967, when bonuses ended and basic pay became more respectable.

One of my very early colleagues of those distant days, who spent many of his holidays bicycling in France, had a very strange housekeeping habit. He sold his vegetable garden produce to his wife, reducing her housekeeping when she dug up potatoes, carrots and the like! What we called him is not for publication!

After maybe two years with Mike Butcher, helping to invest monies for our six investment trusts (now gone the way of all flesh), I went further down (or was it up?) the corridor to join, as the junior, Michael Verey. He really did teach me how to invest the cash assets of wealthy private clients. From this came the introduction into the world of charitable funds and then pension funds – all very much in their infancy at that time. This became the 'specialization' that Mike Butcher had talked about a few years earlier.

Our first pension fund client was the BBC, and the initial paper said it would never exceed £15,000,000 – a huge sum in those days. Today this Fund has seven investment managers, and four property managers, the fund being worth £7,153 million – a real case of little acorns...etc. From those small beginnings, Helbert Wagg became, on its own, one of the leading houses of the day in the management of pension fund assets. We were certainly bigger in this field than were Schroders, but on the amalgamation with them, we were together, as J. Henry Schroder Wagg & Co Ltd, a formidable force.

All of us, young and old, were constantly being lunched out, and even dined out but on my first such occasion I was on the host's left hand. The person on his right hand, being the principal guest, was offered a plate on which sat a large omelette. (I have always asked waiters, 'How much can I take?', because you never know) – my fellow guest took the lot, which was meant for six of us, and confusion and embarrassment reigned. *My* mistake was asking for milk for my coffee – there was none – so now I simply eat and drink what I am given.

Helbert Wagg developed investment management services and was one of the pioneers of institutional fund management after the Second World War. For me it was an accident of timing to have been in the right place at the right time, therefore being in at the beginning of what is now a vast business in many financial centres around the world.

In 1950, for some unknown reason, I was asked by the management of Helbert Wagg if I would like to go to the Second International Banking Conference in Christ Church College, Oxford. It lasted the best part of two weeks, with representatives of banks attending from over forty countries. This was only five years after World War II had ended, and it was surprising how well the different nationalities appeared to get on with each other for most of the time. There was a little tension, usually late in the evenings, between some of the Allies and the Germans and Italians, which did not surprise me. I mention this because Prime Minister Attlee attended our final dinner, and although not expected to give a speech, he was pushed into so doing by all of us drumming the tables until he got to his feet. His speech was only of a few minutes and one comment he made was, 'You all seem to have got on very well together, and as this is so soon after the war, I think it is a great credit to you all. Perhaps the world would be a better place if you ran it and the politicians retired.'

Surely it could be no worse!

When he left, he found that all the tyres of his official car had been let down!

On a personal matter, one event has often been recalled to my mind. In the evenings I would get away from the masses and, as was my custom on these occasions, sit by the river watching the swans and ducks floating past under the light of street lamps from a bridge. A chap came to sit on the other end of the bench whom I took to be a university don. We had a brief discussion about this and that, and seeing his handle-bar moustache, I asked him if he had been in the RAF. He had. As the pow-wow proceeded, I became conscious that he was edging towards me. When his right knee was touching my left one, he asked me what Service I had been in during the War. My answer was, 'The Marines, and if you come one inch nearer you are going in the river.' He left!

Every year, just before Christmas, the staff were called up one by one to see the Managing Director. At Helbert Wagg this was Lionel Fraser, known by the press as 'tall, silver-haired Lionel Fraser'. The discussion ended with a pay rise which, in my case, was beginning to go up in slightly larger lumps, but after our amalgamation, this system rapidly disappeared and letters were handed out. If you were not satisfied, you could seek an interview, and sometimes that worked just a little, but it was always a friendly discussion; the personal touch then still existed.

Alfred Wagg's generosity was well known and, together with Arthur Villiers of Barings, and a partner of Cazenove & Co, they actively and financially supported the Eton Manor Boys Club, an Eton College mission in London's poor East End. They set up a 'penny bank' and every Friday for some years I went to Hackney and collected or paid out these small sums of money (but, remember, a pound then is worth about a penny halfpenny today). That was my first 'voluntary' job. Alfred Wagg also gave 100 acres of Ashdown Forest (The 'Isle of Thorns'), complete with swimming pool and club house, to the Eton Manor Charitable Trust for the use of the boys who were members. The Boy Scouts also benefited from this gesture, and once a year all Helbert Wagg Staff went to the camp for the office party – a very friendly day out and with sufficient time to enjoy it.

It was in 1961/62 that Helbert Wagg amalgamated with Schroders, and together we had a very large portfolio of charitable and pension fund clients, totalling then many hundreds of millions of pounds. As one of the team, still under Michael Verey, we senior members of the Investment Department suddenly found ourselves going off to meetings on our own without directors accompanying us, giving us few men (no ladies in those days) a sudden lift up the ladder.

At one of the early functions, after Schroder Wagg was set up, a social 'get together' was held and the Chairman of the combined Company, Gordon Richardson (later Lord Richardson of Duntisbourne and Governor of the Bank of England) asked me how I thought the amalgamation would go. My response was, 'If we are left to ourselves to work it out, I am sure it will succeed – if we are directed from above, I am not sure because people will leave.' I maintain that the former method was in fact a huge success, whereas the latter would have failed. In my case, I survived until 1973 before being one of the first to leave, and when amalgamations have taken place in many City firms in recent years, we read of individuals and groups of individuals who have often departed within only two or three years, or even less. On more than one occasion it has been proved all too obviously that in City businesses you really are buying the people in them and not the Company – in fact, almost the only asset that financial institutions have is the people, where frequently it is the manager level that really does know the job.

My wife, Cynthia, and I were married in 1952. The ceremony was conducted by Assistant Bishop Jackson of Bath and Wells, who was a friend of my father-in-law, and at a lunch some weeks before the ceremony in Ewell, Surrey, he was emphatic that brides must not be late. In the event, Cynthia was late because the driver confused Cheam Road, Ewell, with Ewell Road, Cheam, and my father-in-law stood in the middle of the road outside his house and flagged down a car which took him and Cynthia to the church. Those in the church, thinking things had started, stood there for some five minutes singing the first hymn, 'O, God our help in ages past' etc, and got to the end before she appeared. We all then sang it a second time and luckily God has helped in the 'years to come.' This is not an irrelevance because in 1961 we lay on the beach in Cornwall and I said to Cynthia, 'We have got to move.' 'Why?' she replied. 'Because when

Our wedding day, 13th October, 1952.
Back row, l-r: Father, Mother, Self, Cynthia, Bishop Jackson, Mother-in-Law, Brother Mick, Father-in-Law.
Front row, l-r: Gill Whitten, Carol Archer, Penny Archer.

Christopher Breach's wedding with Nicola, 1985.

John's wedding to Christine Hood, 1995.

the amalgamation goes through, the one certain thing is that the house-loan scheme will be scrapped.'

Someone certainly watched over us for the ensuing weeks and eventually we found the house in which we still live. Almost the last act in independent Helbert Wagg was one conducted by Michael Verey: my application for a house-loan stated (and I still have it) that when the Board considers the matter, it will be my 20th birthday in the Firm and it will be a nice present. 'What a time to bring this up!' he said, 'How much are you having to pay for it?' '£7750, Sir' (we called our bosses that in 1961). 'What are you buying – a — palace?' he retorted. 'No, Sir,' I said, 'a house in a road I never thought I could afford.' 'I am not at all sure you can,' he said. I got the loan at 3% fixed for 100% of the amount, and the next day they stopped the scheme. If you do not ask, you will not get; if you do ask you just might get, and we, as a family, are immensely grateful to Michael Verey for his help to us, which was, I suppose, a reward for many years' hard work in getting new business and not making too many mistakes.

We did indeed turn in the right direction that day, and when he was in his early 80s, I wrote to him, following a discussion with Tessa Baring, a fellow Trustee of Barnardo's, and sent Verey a copy of the application. I said we were still here. As we shall see later, inflation and the statistics behind it are a sort of hobby, but very germane to the investment of monies. My house is today worth some £500,000, which in real terms has more than kept pace with inflation. I firmly believe in long-termism and the reward from correct investment is discussed later, in Part IV, 'Your Money – How not to lose it.'

The contacts developed on a personal level were, on looking back, quite extraordinary and many of them reappeared in different guises in later years, leading to further new businesses and appointments as a trustee of some of the major charities of England. Again, it is a question of 'who you know' and not necessarily 'what you know', although you have to have a sound knowledge of any relevant subject in order to hold your own with experts in any particular field.

One of the earliest of these connections was with a young stockbroker called Roger Gibbs, later to become Sir Roger Gibbs, the

Chairman of The Wellcome Trust. When Michael Verey was out at lunch one day, I was instructed by a pension fund to purchase £1 million of a gilt-edged security of my choice. This was, in those days, a huge sum of money, and I rang Roger, knowing that his broking firm, De Zoete & Gorton, was one of our favourites of the day. Roger has several times since then told me that he nearly dropped the 'phone because he had never had such an order, and when Verey returned from lunch I told him what I had done. He replied, 'I would not have, but if you have, you have', and that was that. The degree of mutual respect and trust was considerable and I never consulted him again on such matters. Time was of the essence and we all just got on with the job. The learning curve was steep and so, thankfully, were the pay rises that went with it, but in those days, we were not recipients of today's monopoly money payments.

The winning of a client always gives one a satisfactory feeling and in all the years of my City life, in two merchant banks, the losing of one to a competitor is a major disaster that leaves a sinking feeling in one's mind. The loss of a client is not always because of poor investment performance. It was then much more likely to result from the arrival of a new Chairman or Chief Executive of a company, who, for personal reasons, did not like the current investment house, or maybe one of the individuals in it. He might have a favourite of his own, and so make the decision to change managers. Losses will also arise on the amalgamation of companies, and in such cases the losing manager may well have done far better than the winning company's manager, but will nevertheless still lose out. Short-term statistical performance management will also have strange results in the attitude of those in charge, and frequently this is the result of not understanding that quick movements of large sums of monies in restricted markets are not possible. Nevertheless, it did not take me long to realize that the power of any Chairman is immense, and very few Boards of Directors will stand firm and disagree with the boss. But again in the 1950s or 1960s there was much ignorance about performance measurement and mistakes in policy rarely caused the sacking of a manager.

The BBC New Pension Scheme once more comes to mind in this

respect. Investment direction cannot be switched over night. The stock markets could not handle colossal amounts of sales and reinvestments, and the costs of switching were greater in those days than they are today. When one annual discussion took place at the BBC, their then Chairman was Dr Charles Hill (the Radio Doctor). He said to Verey and me, 'It has been a difficult year for you.' We were there for what seemed no more than five minutes, and that was really all that was said. What he should have said was, 'You have not done very well this year and what have you got to say about it?' For some years I was an Honorary Member of the BBC Clubs, so they could not have been too upset.

Fortunately we did not lose the business and over the years we did in fact do very well for them. As mentioned earlier, they now have seven investment and four property managers because of the very size of the fund, and splitting funds is a common feature of today. Wellcome Trust, worth some £15 billion, has some thirty managers world-wide and the annual scrutiny is tough and regular, so there are many more switches of managers than in the past. Quite correctly in many cases.

Many years later, I was again a Trustee, this time of Barnardo's, at a time when Norman Bowie was Chairman. At one investment meeting he said: 'Should we not sack our Investment Management House because they are top of the pops and must fall off the perch before long?' My reply was that this was possibly true, but that it would be a totally outrageous thing to do. No one would understand the logic. On my first visit to Wall Street, an American stockbroker at a conference postulated this theme and said the money should then go to the firm at the bottom of the pile. I can agree that this might well be correct, but I have not yet heard of anyone bold enough to do it.

One of the tricks – if that is the correct word – when managing any pot of money, is to get to know the management of a charity or pension fund on a personal basis. In the early days, after 1948, it was rare for merchant bank directors to visit companies and tour the works; the clients were expected to come to the City. But I am sure that at Helbert Wagg we began to change this. By the 1960s, if I could smell a possible new client, I was totally free to visit the target, be it in Glasgow, Plymouth or anywhere else, and no one ever queried this. One of my first trips away from London included a cold call on The Halifax Building Society, where the then manager (a Mr Potter) gave me a cheque for £1 million to place on deposit, the first such deposit they had ever made with a merchant bank. Another client, The Charities Aid Foundation, was then a small pot of money of some £50,000 and was part of the National Council of Social Services (later The National Council of Voluntary Organizations). Today it has a balance sheet approaching £1 billion. I have been involved with that organization for almost exactly fifty years, partly professionally and partly since retirement, as will be seen in Part III: Work with Charities.

A third similar type of example, already briefly mentioned, is Barnardo's, where I was a Trustee for fifteen years, and this too is enlarged upon in Part III.

When we all came back to the City after the war, a new colleague was David Murison MBE, who was older than I and who had been a Major in the Far East. One day he said to me that Great Britain is run by 1,000 people and I have never forgotten that statement. Michael Verey, possibly in an unguarded moment, once said to me, 'You must know more people in business than anyone I know.' That was coming from him, totally wrong, because he was certainly in that 1,000, but the point is, once again: 'It is the people you know that are important.' The pension fund world, which was beginning rapidly to expand, proved that statement to me in no uncertain way because from 1963 things developed speedily.

I had by then long felt that investing pension fund and charity monies was in a way restricted. Gilt Edged securities and stock market investments in the equity (ordinary shares) market were all that were available. It was almost impossible to invest moneys overseas in those days because of exchange control regulations, and there was the problem of paying a premium to purchase US dollars if one was thinking of buying American shares. This left an obvious glaring blank space, namely the real estate sector. Because of Schroder Wagg's growth in the pension fund management business, I was invited to my first major forum on property matters, the principal lecturer being Norman Bowie, a Fellow of the Royal Institution of Chartered Surveyors, who, over the next thirty years, became a close colleague and friend. He was at that time a partner in Jones Lang Wootton, a major firm of surveyors and real estate managers in London. His lecture was on the subject I had been contemplating for some months, and on the way out I carefully timed my exit so that we met at the door. The conference had been arranged by the stockbrokers, Fielding, Newson Smith & Co, with Dundas Hamilton chairing it. He introduced me to Norman; we swapped cards and within a month he had lunch with me in the City. We exchanged ideas and he told me that two people had already discussed the same idea with him a month or two before, but that he would arrange a meeting if I wished. This was fixed and Cecil Baker, the Chairman elect of the new body and I had a pow-wow in Schroders Building in 1964. He was then at Hambros Bank and we collected some six people who might set the proposed company on its course.

The original idea for this came from Jack Wickert, Pension Manager of Esso Petroleum, and the vehicle was created. We knew that Corporation Tax was to be introduced in 1966 and The Pension Fund Property Unit Trust was started to enable gross funds (Pension funds then paid no tax on dividends because the tax was all reclaimable) to receive rent direct from tenants without losing the reclaimable corporate tax which would have followed from the change in the tax system. The simple explanation of this is: 'Six Pension funds own six buildings next door to each other; if each had a shareholding, there would be a tax loss, but if a gross fund could be set up *owning* all six buildings, then one man could collect the rents and share it out with no tax loss.'

The trust, known always as PFPUT (Pension Fund Property Unit Trust) was the first of its kind, and was some £15 million in six months and way ahead of the competition. The Department of Trade had been involved in a somewhat similar 'co-operative' for Pig Breeding, which had gone bust, and they were scared of a second disaster, so they clamped down on further growth until an enquiry had taken place. They thought that this rapid beginning would lead to an explosion in growth that might get out of control, not realizing, as did we, that the pension movement was then relatively small and that there was, in reality, a ceiling on potential growth. Then, for me, the balloon went up. Gordon Richardson sent for me saying in his own words, 'You have over-egged the pudding, and got the firm into bad odour with the Department of Trade.' Sensing trouble, I had taken an earlier precaution in seeing a new member of Schroder's staff, Sir Leslie Robinson, a retired No 2 at the Department of Trade. He said, 'You have nothing to worry about and you are totally in the clear.' Gordon Richardson then said to me that he was asking Leslie Robinson to join us and I felt like saying 'You can bloody well send for whomsoever you wish,' but I refrained. Leslie came in. Gordon said, 'Barrie says this that and the other', and Leslie replied, 'Barrie is quite right.'

This difficulty is perhaps best described by someone else, and PFPUT had a history written by Richard Redden. Quoting from this, I include the following:-

> Barrie Johnston recalls 'a certain amount' of wrath that Schroders incurred from the Board of Trade. For Johnston himself, the episode brought problems in his relations with Schroders. The directors were at first very concerned that Schroders might be indirectly involved in a dispute with the Board of Trade. It was left to Sir Leslie Robinson to assure the Board and Schroders that the PFPUT idea was sound, safe and quite respectable. The irony of the situation was that at the time, Gordon Richardson was chairman of Schroder Wagg – the man who was later to become Governor of the Bank of England. He had no cause to regret the Schroder involvement as PFPUT was to have no further problems at all with the Board and its successors, the Department of Trade and Industry, and the Department of Trade.
>
> Robinson's intervention with the Board was obviously of the greatest benefit in lifting the fears surrounding PFPUT, and he was told the Board would be re-examining its policy and issuing fresh guidelines. These discussions took place at the end of March 1967, although it was not until August 1967 that PFPUT was permitted to open its doors again. Irritatingly, this was after the Board had already allowed two rival funds to start up.

I do not think I was ever forgiven for this fright to the Schroder board.

PFPUT eventually totalled over £200 million in property for over four hundred pension funds, to be followed by a second such vehicle for Charitable Funds. A third fund, 'The Agricultural Property Unit' Trust came last, and this was a very exciting venture; we eventually owned over 50,000 acres spread across Great Britain from West Wales to Norfolk and Scotland, and in addition, a small vineyard in France – the wine was not very good!

Most of our agricultural land was managed by Cluttons and we knew their partners very well indeed. Many years later, it was Nigel Clutton OBE, then the Chairman of the Mornington Building Society, who invited me to join the Board. That lasted for some four years before the Society was taken over.

Because of the fracas, the nearest I have ever been to being sacked, I was leant upon to press for a second Schroder person, namely a full director, to join the PFPUT board. I refused this notion, saying that PFPUT was independent of the influence of all merchant bank boards. This independence remained even when Sydney Eburne, a director of Morgan Grenfell, joined the PFPUT board. His merchant bank had also placed many pension fund clients into the vehicle. Sydney later retired on his appointment as Chairman of the Crown Estates, and later received a Knighthood for his services.

This policy of independence proved in the end to be a great success, but it was a near squeak for me. It always amazes me to see on TV programmes the commonly held view that merchant banking is easy and a bit of a pushover. This is very far from the truth, and when I went to Charterhouse Japhet later on, I had some twelve years on the Board before retirement, with only two of us surviving that length of time. Tough but fun – for some!

A second idea when at Schroders was the formation of a Life Assurance Company. We did get one off the ground, with three foundation directors: the Chairman was Gordon Popham, a very clever investment manager, now, sadly, deceased, David Walters, an actuary, now elsewhere, and me – also elsewhere. Schroder Life Assurance Company Ltd gave us much interest and a great struggle to get it off the ground, and it was eventually sold to an Australian Insurance Company. Two years after its formation, I left to join Charterhouse Japhet as a Director.

One reason for leaving Schroders after just short of thirty-two years was a personality clash with one of the senior directors, who had better be nameless. This difference of opinion arose possibly because we managed the Pension Fund of Boots, where Michael Verey was a non-executive director. Their pension fund manager, Harold Chave-Jones, then on the Council of the National Association of Pension Funds, asked me to give a paper to the annual conference on inflation, which happened to be a sort of personal hobby. I naturally asked the Board member of Schroders for permission to give it and permission got bogged down. In the end I was told, 'Why have you been asked and not me?' I bluntly replied something to the effect that I knew what I wanted to say and that if he gave the lecture I would have to write it for him. I never received the formal OK, but gave it nevertheless, a black mark which stopped further promotion. A very good friend on Schroders Board was Ashley Ponsonby (now Sir Ashley Ponsonby), who once said, 'You are a bloody fool to stop here. Whilst one man is here, you will get no further.' When I gave in my notice to him six months' later he said, 'You lucky bugger – how did you pull that off?' So I went to Charterhouse in 1972 and had no regrets whatever, but was nevertheless sad that the parting of the ways after so many years had to happen. In the end, when shaving every morning, you have to face yourself in the mirror and the thought of seeing a reflection every morning knowing that I had been 'chicken' forced the issue.

The second reason, thus triggering eventual departure, was the promotion to full Board level of some five people younger than I by many years – as many as fifteen in a few cases. Michael Verey knew I was far from happy about this and arranged for me to see Gordon Richardson. We had quite a stiff discussion and at one point I said, 'Have you moved the goal posts and therefore am I beyond the winning post?' The answer left me in little doubt that this was so, and I then debated the problem at length with my wife Cynthia, who has always been a good listener, and a wise counsel – she had in fact been saying for a year or more that I should look elsewhere. So plans had to be laid. By one of those chances in life, I went with some pension fund managers to British Motor Corporation in Longbridge to discuss that Company with their Board. I had, for some time, managed the pension fund portfolio of Standard Motor Company and Schroders were the mastermind behind putting Leyland Motors (I also managed that fund) into the BMC business. We also knew Lord Stokes well. On the way back to London in a special Pullman Car, I sat opposite Christopher Taylor-Young, then a director of Hill Samuel. We both let our hair down over a drink when we discovered that we had exactly the same attitude to our own personal situations.

Soon after that, he left Hill Samuel and went to Charterhouse Japhet as a Director, to head up the Investment Department, hopefully to build a new Pension and Charity investment management business. I telephoned him, reminded him of our train journey and said I was now looking to move. He instantly replied, 'You've got a job here – come round.' I put the phone down, walked round the corner, saw him and did indeed get the job, subject to their Board agreement.

The final hurdle was a lunch at Charterhouse with some of the Board, and it was chaired by Hilton Clark, who had been head of the Discount Office of the Bank of England and had been appointed to Charterhouse by the Bank of England on his retirement from that organization. He was of immense stature in the City and a much respected and likeable man. He said to me, 'You have an interesting hobby – tell me about it.' He referred to my collection of gold sovereigns (all sold a year or so ago!), which I had started to buy at £4 each, and in this discussion my comments alluded to the step-by-step fall in sterling with sudden Treasury decisions to devalue our currency from time to time. 'What would you do?' he said. My answer was emphatic in that it is useless to hold currencies at fixed levels, at a huge cost to any country's reserves, and that sterling should be floated. Apparently he must have agreed because my appointment was confirmed and I went there in September 1972 to an empty desk and all to play for.

On leaving Schroders, two very nice and totally unexpected things happened. The first was being invited back to Schroders some two months later to join a farewell party for me, which I accepted, providing, in my own words, 'You pay the bill not me!' It was then customary for 'leavers' to pay for their own party, while retirees attended as guests!

A vast number of people, who by that time were ex-colleagues, attended and again Michael Verey featured. He had been at a meeting at the Bank of England and left it, to return later, after making a very generous statement about my work over so many years and ending by giving me a sizeable cheque, which, for once, took my breath away. I was told afterwards that I was the first person ever to receive such a parting gift, and one of the Board, another very good friend, told me later that it had made him spit because when he left he had got nothing! A guilty conscience I wonder on someone's part, but the cheque did its trick – it pays to speak one's mind at all times, I believe, and I repeat my first Royal Marines bit of advice: if you are asked a question, answer it truthfully – you'll sleep better on it. You really do. So ended thirty-one years and ten months of extraordinary growth at Helbert Wagg/Schroder Wagg, where the investment philosophy (or was it my own philosophy which happened to agree?) set the scene for a pay-off later. With the cheque I was given, my wife and I bought a much needed new gas cooker for the kitchen and the rest went into the stock market, all in ordinary shares. It is still there, maybe in different shares, and vastly improved in value.

This left PFPUT without a Schroder representative and again two pleasant things happened. Tom Biggs (also sadly now deceased), the Hoover Pension Fund Manager, wrote to Cecil Baker, the PFPUT Chairman, recommending that I should stay on the Board in my own right and this was agreed by all my colleagues – a very pleasant and totally unexpected gesture. The second thing was that Schroders appointed Arthur Green to take my place – he had recently retired from the Legal & General, where he had been the senior property man, and as I had to repay my house mortgage, then secured with the Legal & General on favourable terms, on leaving Schroders, I asked him if he would help me to get a personal 'with profits' policy to cover the loan at the then going rate of around 6%. This was eventually agreed, and I have their letter which stated 'that in no circumstances, repeat no circumstances, will such a request be granted again.' They had not wanted me to pay the extra premium and make a hoped-for capital gain on my house as well as a profit from their investment services. I did, to the tune of a £10,000 cheque when the mortgage was paid off, which was considerably more than the original mortgage of £5,750, and by then the house was worth some £250,000! It has doubled since then, as I have already mentioned.

The pension fund annual conferences were very well organized, being held in the early days in big hotels in, for example, Bournemouth, Brighton and the spa towns of England. Later it moved to Southern Ireland in Killarney and to Monte Carlo. The participants were mostly stockbrokers, merchant bankers, actuaries and of course pension fund managers. The debates and seminars were at a very high level of professional understanding of the subjects of the day, and it has taken too many years for governments of all political colours around the world to understand that, whereas in the UK in 1900 there were nine people working to one retired person, there are now somewhere around 2.5 people working to one retired. All countries face a huge problem in trying to balance the books and that is why at last we are beginning to grasp the problem with the publication in September 2000 of the fact that quite large numbers of young people are starting to put money aside for their old age. Most State pensions are paid out of unfunded schemes, and the increasing costs looming on the horizon are getting serious and will, in the end, be impossible to honour, as we are beginning to understand.

The evening sessions at the conferences were one long round of cocktail parties and, after dinner, even more parties that went on well beyond normal bedtime. This particularly applied in Killarney, where things were very Irish indeed. Conference sessions were meant to start at 9.00 am, but early morning tea never arrived before that time; the whole programme was torn apart by breakfast being over an hour late. Nevertheless, it all helped everyone to swap ideas and occasionally to switch investment managers. My first such success was with the Solicitors Clerks Pension Fund and others followed, including Allied Breweries and Tarmac. As the years progressed, so did the professionalism and this led to the formation of the Pensions Management Institute in 1976. One of my actuary friends was Terry Arthur, who had played rugby for England, and when the Institute set up the machinery for competing papers for an annual prize, we wrote a paper together and in so doing he taught me a great deal about how to write such a document. We won the first prize ever given and following that event, the Council elected me a Fellow in 1978, this being an elevation from Associate. I could not help but think about leaving Epsom College with only three equivalent 'O' levels in 1941 and of Winston Churchill, who also never passed an exam. Today it is a much more difficult world in which to progress up a ladder without academic degrees, and I think this is a pity because everyone develops at different speeds and sitting exams is not the favourite pastime of many people – I am no exception. In one of my discussions with Gordon Richardson at Schroders we once debated this lack of academic qualification at a time when we had a large intake of graduates. When I said, 'the war was my university', he sportingly said, 'I will give you that one.'

Staff moving between merchant banks in the 1950s was rare because the 'old boys' club' worked well and it was not unknown for a chairman of a company to telephone another one to say that he had a member of staff from the latter's firm who was looking for a job. When the decision was made to leave Schroders, I did see Kenneth Keith (later Sir Kenneth), then the chairman of Hill Samuel. This introduction was made by the doyen of the pension world, the late George Ross Goobey. When Keith asked could he talk to Verey, I said he could, because I knew Verey would not be surprised, but I decided not to go down that path. Even more surprising, when talking to another merchant bank, was the statement, 'You can come here with pleasure, but it is not you.' This was a truly friendly comment and one which, later on, I was more than grateful to have received, and of which I did take notice. That Company eventually went out of business, so neither turning left nor right was the correct decision on that occasion.

Chapter Two

Charterhouse

One of the first internal appointments at Charterhouse followed my first meeting with the Group Chairman, Derek Wylde. He said that he knew I was heavily involved in pension funds and that he wished to appoint me to the Group Pension Fund Board, and would I consider the paper on reducing the retirement age from sixty-five to sixty-three or sixty-two. The cost of such a reduction is considerable and my comment was that if such a thought was a possibility, they should bite the bullet and cut it to sixty-two, because I had no doubt that in the space of years it would be cut to sixty, and so it was. Today it seems to me that very few merchant bank, bank or insurance company personnel, of whatever level, will stay the course to reach even sixty – early retirement has a dramatic effect on pension payments, cutting expected payments, in many cases, by more than 5% a year – i.e. if retirement takes place at fifty rather than the expected sixty, there could be a 50% reduction in one's anticipated pension and, of course, one would miss pay rises over those ten years which would have increased the pension. Capital payments on 'loss of office' are, more often than not, nowhere near the benefit they seem at first sight, in spite of the temptation to receive a large cheque. One should lock up an increased pension rather than taking cash and a reduction in pension.

Growth at Charterhouse Japhet, the merchant banking arm of the Group, began to escalate in several directions. One was the opening of branch offices in Birmingham, Manchester, Edinburgh and Cardiff. A second was the formation of a life insurance company, and the third was opening an office in Jersey – I had tried to get Schroders to do this but failed, although they did set up shop there many years later.

The regional offices were, in a way, the listening posts for our original business of helping small private companies up and down the country, as well as being catalysts for winning new businesses. The operation consisted, if we thought fit, of putting up equity capital perhaps to the tune of say 40% plus a small amount of loan capital; the reverse, to some extent, of the way the Industrial Commercial Finance Corporation (ICFC) operated, by putting up larger slices of loan capital but smaller amounts of equity capital. Each local office had its own Managing Director, not necessarily a member of the Charterhouse Japhet Board, and I was a Director of all of them as a Main Board Director. This necessitated frequent rail journeys to meetings, long days, and stays away from home. I had a rule about nights away: if in the United Kingdom I telephoned home and spoke to Cynthia every night; if out of the country, every third night, when in our offices in New York, Philadelphia or Houston.

It was on one of the early trips to Manchester that, travelling in the Pullman train, I was literally the occupant of the last seat for breakfast (always the best meal on the railways). The waiter came along and said, 'There are two things about being last, Sir.' 'What are they?' I replied. 'You either get none or two.' I had one and a half!

On a return journey one afternoon from Birmingham with my colleague, Lionel Anderson, the guard started us off and said, 'May Allah be with us.' He was – we had a brick thrown through the window when going at about 100mph, and luckily it missed both of us. Allah be praised!

The opening of the Jersey business was the result of another opportunity that came out of the blue. We had won the pension management account of Bristol Street Motors. The Company had several tentacles in the motor car business apart from that of selling new and secondhand cars in the Midlands. It made seats for aeroplanes, children's harnesses to fit on the seats of cars, and also designed the galleys of passenger airplanes, which most people nowadays are so used to seeing. To help finance more cheaply the raising of cash to pay for the cars, Bristol Street had a very small finance house in Jersey, staffed by one man and a secretary. The office in Hill Street was possibly the smallest building in the road, and although respectable to the eyes on the ground floor, the structure on the upper floor(s) was decidedly dodgy. When trading conditions were tough in the motor trade, the Chairman, Harry Cressman, said one evening in his home that he thought he would sell the Jersey office because it had had its day. This seemed an incredible 'accident of fate' and I could hardly believe my ears. Although not trying to seem too keen, it was agreed that if I could convince the Charterhouse Japhet Board, I would like to go to Jersey to see what could be made of such a tiny operation. That visit, my first to the island, was the beginning of trips every three weeks or monthly. It lasted for several years. We paid (and this is memory) something like £15,000 to purchase the business, and after several meetings with Colin Powell, the head of Jersey's finance division of their 'Civil Service', we obtained a licence to start a banking business to be used by overseas customers, etc. On repeated trips over the early months, I was pressured by him from time to time as to why we were not building it up quickly enough for him (that was what I thought he meant anyway!) and repeatedly, at the beginning I said I did not really know how we were going to develop things satisfactorily for him, but we would do our best. Slowly this happened and we had to set up a Board of Directors on which the preponderance of the Board had to be Jersey residents. This was also done, and there were three locals, one being Senator Dick Shenton, with two of us from Charterhouse. Apart from myself, the other London person was John Sleeman, an extremely clever man who had great knowledge of law and an amazing capacity for turning out sizeable minutes and paper in seemingly a matter of hours. For some years we alternated acting as Chairman, but for the last four or five years before my retirement in 1984, I filled that role.

Building something from nothing is, for me, much more interesting and certainly more fun than simply managing something. And following the normal business of pension fund management, this was the third creation of a new venture, following those of Schroder Life Assurance and the Pension Fund Property Unit Trust. I suppose my role in Jersey lasted some ten years, and over that time we moved offices twice. When the third move was mooted, my time began to come to an end and I never saw it completed, although I did visit afterwards, when doing a job for the Halifax Building Society. This connection was created way back in the years and it was after my final retirement from full-time City work that the then Finance Director of the Halifax asked me to do a research job for him and arrange some meetings, particularly with the Jersey senior Civil Servant, Colin Powell, mentioned earlier. They eventually set up their own offices. Two stories about the personalities in Jersey which amuse me even now often come to mind, and again past connections come back into the picture. The first Commandant General, Royal Marines whom I had met after the war was General Sir Peter Whiteley (mentioned earlier for being colour-blind), and he held that very senior position when I first went back to Deal Barracks as a member of the Royal Marines Association. That would have been around 1972, and when he retired from that high office, he was appointed Governor of Jersey and kindly agreed to visit our tiny office in Hill Street. He talked to every one of our staff, possibly six or seven in all, and after that we went to luncheon to meet all the other Board members and VIP guests. When we got into the car, he said something like, 'You know the routine – I acknowledge people on my right and you take the left.' I don't think we actually acknowledged anyone, but we had a meaningful lunch. The visit was for us a pleasant occasion and helped to put our small office on the map.

The second set of memories was in fact two, both with Senator Shenton. He invited me to his Silver Wedding party and I thought that was a most generous gesture on his part. It was an evening dinner and it seemed to me that apart from his family and friends, I was the only 'outsider.' We had many interesting discussions both in and out of the office for many years, and he also added stature to our small set-up. The second particular memory of him concerned a much more serious matter: the British Government introduced VAT on dealing in gold, and this affected gold coins. Charterhouse Japhet in London were very large dealers in bullion, sovereigns and Kruger Rands to the tune of many tens of millions of pounds a year, and we took this skill to Jersey, which was free of such tax. At an early Board Meeting after the announcement I said that I felt there would be a distinct chance that smuggling might ensue. Dick Shenton was horrified and said immediately that he did not want to be part of any enquiries that might happen in the future if our customers were caught in such a racket, and that he would resign at once. We pleaded with him not to do such a thing, arguing that it was up to us to enforce strong rules so as to prevent any such happening. We did just that immediately, and he stayed! The one precaution that stopped such an event occurring was the decision never again to open accounts for people who came into the bank with cases full of notes. We only accepted cheques drawn on other banks and when we found one of our competitors did get into a spot of bother (£8 million from memory) a few years later, we were in the clear.

Visiting Jersey became a pleasure and I nearly always had the same room in The Longueville Manor. It was far enough away from the office to ensure that the excess of eating from which one suffered could be walked off. On each of my trips home I brought back a litre of whisky, and on one occasion, when getting out of the plane at Gatwick, I tripped on the way up the stairs and smashed a full bottle of Glenmorangie Malt. I have often wondered whether I threw away £8 or £16 – or whatever was the then difference between Jersey and UK prices. In my last two years as Chairman we had made a profit of some £250,000 a year – not bad from a £15,000 investment!

Having created Schroder Life Assurance a few years earlier, I knew something about Life Companies, and John Sleeman and I were again involved in a new venture, but this time he was Chairman from start to finish. We converted, or perhaps it is more accurate to say he converted, a small in-house company which had been set up for our own pension funds, into something much larger. This also was quite exciting and later we had, as an outside director, John Cudworth, the Managing Director of Refuge Assurance Company of Liverpool. The first step in enlargement was the taking over of an insurance broking company whose Managing Director joined our board. For a reason which was irrelevant, John Sleeman was absent for the next two board meetings. At the first of these meetings I asked the newcomer to produce some figures for us at the next meeting. He did not and I for one was hopping mad, saying in no uncertain terms that his lack of action was totally out of order and that he would hear further from us. An enquiry then ensued because he seemed evasive and, cutting this story short, he never appeared again and he lost his house and his car into the bargain. Our insurance company was eventually sold to the Refuge, and John Sleeman quite rightly joined their Board – it was a prestigious appointment, but sadly it did not last long for John because he died suddenly very soon after.

One other example of disobeying orders and getting away with it was when Charterhouse was involved in a large new issue for Argyll, the supermarket business. This was a big operation for us which was done jointly with another merchant bank and, perhaps exceptionally, we had retained a rather larger slice of the underwriting than was normal – this was because no risk could be seen on the horizon and a little extra profit would be acceptable. But, risk there suddenly was because, out of the blue, the country had an unexpected major problem on its hands and stock market prices suffered a nasty setback. The shock to the system was the Argentinians landing on the Falkland Islands. Our bank chairman, Malcolm Wells, was away; Christopher Taylor Young was also missing, and the Deputy Chairman and I were suddenly face to face in the passage. Victor Blank asked what the share price was and I told him. 'Sell our allotment' was his instruction and knowing that the loss would have been the best part of £100,000, I said I refused to do it. Having been involved in similar, but less dramatic events before, I felt that markets would recover and that we would eventually reduce our paper loss. In the event, as always happens, prices did recover and we got out without loss. Thanks were never given on that occasion, but that is what one is paid for and relationships were never strained. Part of the game, I call it, and I can assure you that that sort of thing really does make the adrenaline flow quicker than normal. Fortunately for one's health, these occasions are rather rare, and even once every couple of years would have to be put down to bad management rather than bad luck.

One point that was, and probably still is, standard practice at merchant banks relates to fees earned from outside directorships. It is obvious that these activities take you away from your office and when absent you are therefore not using your time for the good of the Company. Accordingly, those outside fees are, correctly, handed over to your principal employer and I had no problem with that; what is happening though is that those relatively few people who are in this lucky position can switch off from internal politics by doing these other things. There is also a huge benefit, if you play the cards correctly, in retaining those outside posts when retiring from a merchant bank, because then the fees can be paid into your own account – but more of this later.

Charterhouse Group had several different facets to its operations, one being the Bank and others being the insurance broking business of Glanville Enthoven, a varied group of industrial companies, and an interest in oil which was of quite some importance, this being based in Aberdeen. Because of its oil activities, we opened an office in Houston, Texas and although small by international standards, it did make quite an impact on our network of connections. The annual visit to New York, Boston and Washington was now extended to Houston, and took on average ten days. We bought a house for the Bank in Houston where the local Managing Director from London lived and visitors could relax away from isolation in big hotels. On one visit to Houston, Cynthia (who came with me on a few occasions) and I were invited to the famous River Oaks Club for dinner, and there we could have had a minor upset. When we were called for dinner, we were halfway through cocktails and on rising to our feet, we were not allowed to take our drinks with us; the waiters put them on silver trays and escorted us to the table, and once seated, we were handed back the glasses. The point about this was that all the club members were white and all the waiters black. Cynthia was somewhat shocked about this, and I really do not know if she would have gone again if asked, but we were not, and so a diplomatic incident was averted. I wonder if the rules have changed since then.

It was after one of these round-the-houses trips that my then Chairman of the Bank asked me 'Where the hell have you been?' I said, 'to America,' and he asked me how long I had been away. I replied, 'a month – ten days business and twenty days holiday.' 'How the devil can you go away for a month?' Answer: 'There is a telephone, and if I came back for a board meeting and then went on three weeks holiday you would not say anything would you?' He did not ask me again, but by spending four weeks a year, much of it in the sticks, you really do get the feel of political and financial practices in that great country, and I like America and the Americans anyway.

Towards the end of my years at Charterhouse, several things happened through all these connections. Glanville Enthoven, now no longer in existence, asked me if I knew anyone at Lincoln's Inn because they were seeking to increase their insurance business. By another coincidence, I knew well the Under Treasurer, Lt. Col Robin Bridges, a retired Royal Marines Officer who had been a Captain Instructor at the RMOCTU in Thurlstone Hotel when I was being put through the hoops so many years before. Glanvilles got the business, and later Robin became the Chairman of the Royal Marines Association for a few years of my thirty years or so on Council, for all of which I had been the Honorary Treasurer.

At one of my early RMA Annual General Meetings in 1972 I met again one of my 'old comrades' who attended and who was then a full Colonel – he was John Wilcox, who later became the Agent for (Sir) Peter Hordern, the Conservative Member of Parliament for Horsham. Peter had been another of the many stockbrokers with whom I had had almost daily contact for many years. John Wilcox had been in my room as an officer cadet in Deal in 1943/44 and a third member of the six of us was Tim Travers-Healy (later Professor) who succeeded brilliantly as an academic and businessman. He beat me to receiving an OBE and again, by coincidence, Tim is a member of The Athenaeum Club in London, where the Charities Aid Foundation has from time to time held small lunches for retiring Trustees and senior staff. Tim and I have afterwards gossiped about the past at length, but what happened to the other three I do not know – I cannot now remember even their names!

In building up the investment department at Charterhouse, we much needed additional talent, and after two – or was it three? – efforts, we tempted away from Schroders a person who had originally been seconded to Helbert Wagg many years before, when he was a 'boy' at Standard & Chartered Bank. He spent some months with us and returned to his Bank, only to reappear as a member of Schroder Wagg staff some time later. He was (and still is) Lionel Anderson, a quiet but brilliant investor who has made a great impression on others. He helped considerably in winning and keeping clients and after some years, as his retirement was nearing, I was able to get him appointed to the investment committee of The Charities Aid Foundation, where I chaired that committee. We have worked together one way or another for some thirty years or so, and he has taken my place as an Honorary Consultant to the Royal Navy and Royal Marines Dependent Relatives Fund, and has followed me as Hon Adviser to the Royal Marines on investment matters as well. This is still a valued friendship and only this year, 2000, has he finally retired – to study local history in Tunbridge Wells. His other activities include Himalayan walking with his wife Shirley.

Because of my many visits to the United States, a London stockbroker introduced me to a Canadian citizen who had advised one of the candidates who was aiming at being the Premier in a Canadian Election. He had very many connections and he had set up in Washington DC a company called 'The Government Research Corporation'. It was a lobbying body and it lasted some five or six years before it closed down, but for all of that time I was more than fortunate in being appointed to help find financial experts who could come – at some expense I would add – to an annual conference in Washington DC. This event was of an exceptionally high order and over the years my recruits included the Chief Executive of one of our clearing banks, the Finance Director of the BBC, the Financial Director of the Halifax Building Society, the Chairman of Glynwed, the Chief Executive of The Refuge Assurance Company and others of that position in similar bodies. Apart from being paid, Cynthia joined me at those conferences in order to help in the entertaining that goes with such an event. These covered luncheon and evening functions where similar people from most of the financial centres of the world were also present, most of them with their wives.

The visits that we made during the four days each year included sessions of some one hour each with the Chairman of the World Bank, an afternoon in The Pentagon, visits to the working departments of the White House, the US Budget Office and the like. The *pièce de résistance* was undoubtedly the final dinners which were held on the top floor of the US State Department – a great privilege. The setting was quite superb, with a floodlit view of the Senate at night, the internal surroundings consisting of the finest of antique furniture and pictures, and, of course, top quality food and wines. On the other evenings, we had such events as a boat trip on the Potomac River followed by a visit to General Washington's house at Mount Vernon. On other occasions we had dinner in the Space Museum and at one such dinner the principal speaker was Senator John Glenn, who, it will be remembered was one of the first men in space. Other similar events were enjoyed. At those functions we were totally free to talk to any of the American politicians who were guests and how different they were from our own British Ministers! When discussing points in England, I have never found Members of Parliament admit, in trying to answer questions, that they do not know. They usually talk on and hedge round the question, but it was quite a shock, and a pleasant surprise in Washington, to hear Senators and Members of the House of Representatives say they did not know and they would find out the answers to questions. This may seem a bit too emphatic, but it is my experience, and I ask you who may read this, if you have ever heard parliamentarians say they 'do not know.' The person whom I met more than once on these occasions was Senator Bob Dole, who was always extremely frank, and it was a real pleasure to see him over those years and to hear face to face how he viewed the difference in the systems of Government in the USA versus Great Britain. He said that he would give anything to have an Opposition as we do, whereby when a Government is defeated, the successors can take office the next day, and all the positions of office are almost all known before the event because of our system of having a Shadow Cabinet. In his own words, when a President changes, every post becomes vacant, and the new incumbent has to appoint even his own barber! My response was that we could take a leaf out of their book and employ experts who can participate on their respective subjects rather than listening to Members of Parliament who pretend they can answer any question put to them – be it atomic energy, agriculture, defence, finance or whatever. No one knows everything about everything, and I believe electors would have a great deal of respect for cabinet members who could honestly say 'I do not know – I will find out and let you know.'

It was trips like these, as well as business trips for my bank, that enabled Cynthia and me to travel privately so often in the vast countries that are the United States and Canada. When air travel is 'paid for' one by the companies on whose behalf the travel over the 'pond' takes place, it really does reduce the cost of a holiday. Over the years we have driven more than 50,000 miles in those two countries, several times when elections were taking place, and given that the television is nowhere near the standard of UK television, it presents great opportunities to switch off the box and join the local residents in their favourite 'chop shops'. Two or three weeks every year does give one a real picture of life in the mountains and plains of these two countries, where population is sparse indeed. On two occasions in these areas we have driven the best part of 100 miles and never seen another car – imagine travelling from London to Birmingham and not seeing another car!

Just one funny incident is worth recording; it amuses me anyway. To get off a freeway when travelling from Grand Canyon to Los Angeles, we turned off and took the only other road that went in the same direction. After a couple of hours, seeing no other form of life, we stopped at a tin hut where petrol was being sold and the attendant came out. The conversation went like this:

Me: 'Will you please fill the tank'
Him: Yup
Me: It is very hot today (100° or so)
Him: Yup
Me: Does the railroad work
Him: Yup
End of conversation.

There was nothing, absolutely nothing, for some fifty miles on either side of this hut except sand.

A few years later when travelling the same road in the reverse direction, we came across the hut again – burnt out and no one in sight. Perhaps the conversation drove him away! But the point of this aside is that when getting out into the 'sticks', it makes one realize that the 'cities' are not America, and that one can understand why news on local radio and in local papers never seems to cover more than a radius of fifty miles. When Margaret Thatcher won her first election, it was never mentioned anywhere where we were – I had to 'phone my son in England to find out the result. So investors take note: it is a different environment and beware of salesmen. This subject is tackled later, so read on.

The first-hand knowledge obtained on these multifarious trips was invaluable, both positively and negatively, and again I refer to the decisions to be made about turning left or right.

Merchant banks, in common with all companies of whatever type, have the world in which to seek out clients, and one stockbroker, no longer in existence I am afraid, organised two trips to South Africa to see if his own connections would be interesting enough for us to invest in that country. Everything being equal, which it never is, the answer ought to be 'yes', but of course politics and racial problems are major considerations and the outlook some twenty years ago was not as good as it might appear to some today, even though today most people may still say 'No'. South Africa has virtually all the minerals and precious metals that are needed in modern industry; it has great wine-growing facilities and so on, and her citizens are not slow in advertising the values of the holiday trade. In my two visits of a month in all, I was shocked – and I think that that is the correct word – to see so many factories of American, German, French and Italian companies, but very few British ones. Whether that has changed for the better I do not know. If it has we were late in starting. If it has not, we have either made a good decision or missed a trick. My gut feeling is still that putting large sums of money in developing countries presents considerable risks, but at some stage the huge difference between advanced nations and those left way behind simply has to be put right, and I would rather see governments in preference to companies take action, where the risk is often too great for investors and the time span too long.

Some of my own companies looked and said no, and now a few of them are themselves being taken over by South African companies. Why is it that the grass always looks greener over the fence when more often than not it turns out to be full of weeds – or did we fail to select correctly? All this is part of the background to my investment philosophy, which from now on plays a major part in my life and, thankfully, most of my clients and friends can say 'thank you' and mean it. That does not mean to say that one could not have done better; of course with hindsight we all could have done better, but at least the negatives, which could have been a hell of a lot worse, thankfully did not fall into that category.

My interest in property was extended first of all by joining The Property & Finance Luncheon Club in the City of London, which had been created by David Pickford, the chief executive of Haslemere Estates. PFPUT shared a very large development with this company many years later, when we re-developed the large site at the southern end of Richmond Bridge. My Schroder Wagg colleague, John White, had joined the Club at its creation, but because he was not interested in property, he said I should take his place and this duly happened. The purpose of the Club was to hold some four or five lunches a year and it was envisaged that the membership should, if possible, be split between property people and financial people. Soon after joining, the job of Honorary Treasurer was vacated and I fell into the position, which I held for some ten years. During that period the most extraordinary thing occurred. We used to lunch in the early years at the Junior Carlton Club in Pall Mall and, quite exceptionally, we had two lunches in the space of some six weeks, the second being just before our own financial year end. I received the bill for the second lunch and paid it, leaving the first outstanding in our accounts. Six months then passed and I telephoned the Junior Carlton Club, which was in the process of closing its doors. The first bill has been paid, they said. 'Not by me', was my response and it took ages to find out that a stockbroking firm had had a couple of lunches there as well and that they had paid it! It was no good me doing anything about this because they also had gone bust in the meantime. We kept the outstanding amount of some £600 in our books for five or six years, and after seven years it was slowly consumed to the benefit of the then current members. Sloppy management in both places seemed to be coincidental, but it was at a time when brokers were so busy that this sort of thing did happen. It was even known that some scurrilous people used to present spurious bills to companies, and that many were actually paid. One cannot but wonder what auditors were doing when this sort of thing was known to be happening and why management was not on the lookout. The senior partner, whom I never told about this, was a fellow commuter and his son was a well known motorcar racer, and in his youth was a member of my sports club. Both are now sadly deceased, but nevertheless will not be named by me. When people say to me that I appear to trust no one, I usually reply that when it comes to money, I do not, and in both my merchant banks and one public company I have seen one colleague from each spend time behind bars – very sad but nevertheless true. By being vigilant in each case, we were able to get back all the misappropriated money before it reached too large a figure.

During my years at Charterhouse, the Corporate Finance Department from time to time launched on to the Stock Market what had been private companies, and it is customary when such events take place to have a celebratory luncheon or dinner to mark the occasion. There is nothing out of the ordinary on these occasions, but one particular day is one that always amuses me and in the end netted me a sizeable financial gain and an equally sizeable missed opportunity. The company in question was a chemical company from up north and I sat opposite one of their non-executive directors. We discussed nothing in particular but something he said made me say, in one of those moments of total and sudden silence, that I had often thought of putting some money into wine. He very quickly said that he was a director of a wine company and asked 'how much do you want to spend?' I had not the slightest idea of what was thought a reasonable figure but did know what my bank manager would lend me without reference to him. I answered, 'Is £1,500 too little?' (this was in 1972) and if not, what is a sensible start.' He replied that this was a very good beginning and he helped me select 650 bottles of claret and port, most of it not his company's, but from Berry Bros & Rudd. He said, 'If you want a good start, buy their stuff.' It was all kept in their cellars for an annual fee and I landed up with 160 bottles of A1 port and the rest in goodish claret, about which I knew nothing – but have learned a little since then.

Nothing was drunk for ten years and then slowly we drew down some of the claret. It was never my intention to drink the port because once a bottle is opened, it should really be drunk in a day or two and I could not see this happening in my house. Cutting the story short, we eventually drank about half the claret and sold all the rest of it and all the port for over £6,000. That was the good news some twenty years later and it was nearly all put back into more claret at £30 a bottle – now it would cost £100 a bottle and it will last ten more years at the current slow consumption rates. But now comes a different story and you can judge for yourselves whether I won or not.

A very good restaurant in the City, now sadly long gone, was a venue for my guests from time to time and, again, knowing nothing about wine, I found what I thought was a good one and after perhaps some five or six lunches with the same wine over the ensuing weeks, I asked the Maitre d' if I could purchase a case. 'Certainly,' he replied and I paid him something like £25-£30 (in 1972, remember). He told me that he visited his uncle in Dorking every Saturday and that as he virtually passed my door he would drop it in. It lay in a cupboard in the dark for over twenty-five years and I said to my wife that we had better drink it before it went off. So over a spell of twelve months we did just that, bar one bottle which was not quite right. The following Christmas, looking at Berry Bros list, I saw 1962 Lynch Bages Pauillac Premier Cru at the price of £360 a bottle. We had drunk some £4,000 and when I 'phoned Berry Bros to tell them what we had done, the gentleman said, 'I trust you enjoyed it, Sir.' I replied that I did, but I was not quite sure I had enjoyed it *that* much – you win some you lose some!

It was from about the middle of the 1970s that my involvement with the charity world began to escalate from what had been small beginnings. In the two merchant banks I have mentioned, the investment background to my business life, and many of the clients, were universities, hospitals, charitable trusts such as Balliol College,

The Beit Trust, Bedford College for Women, The Royal College of Obstetricians and Gynaecologists, The Royal College of Nurses, The Royal College of General Practitioners etc. These bodies really do focus one's mind on what money is all about. They are not like pension funds, where new money is flowing in almost daily, but are pots of money which, by and large, can only increase by successful investment management. One surgeon said to me, 'We are only medics, you know, and we don't understand money,' to which, after looking at their balance sheet and profit and loss account, my reply was, 'That is obvious.' Helping bodies such as these is immensely interesting and it is the interest and involvement that I have found at all times to be the motivating factors. Today my fear is that the younger generation simply has not got the time to become involved as volunteers in the management problems of their clients – they work for professional firms, as did my generation, but time spent away from offices on clients' domestic matters is non-profit making and so the hands-on interest has gone out of the proverbial window. This will be debated later at greater length.

St Paul's Cathedral and The George Cross
A final story about Charterhouse is well worth recording. Merchant Bankers are not slow in sponsoring music events, sports activities, art exhibitions and similar events because they invite their important clients to attend as guests to what are, in effect, well aimed 'advertising' functions. In our case, we did something different in 1984, just before I retired, and I give top marks to my colleague Christopher Taylor-Young for having such a splendid idea.

Our offices were in St Paul's Cathedral churchyard and Christopher and I had rooms facing this superb Wren building. For some years we had watched work proceeding on cleaning the stonework and replacing some of the fabric which had decayed. We learned that the holder of the George Cross, formerly Royal Engineer Sapper George Wyllie, was going to auction his George Medal, awarded for his effort in digging out an unexploded bomb which the Germans had dropped in 1940 between the Cathedral and our offices. On hearing this, Christopher suggested to the Board that we should purchase it and give it to the Cathedral. We purchased the George Cross for £12,000 in 1984 and it rests in the Crypt for all to see. This donation was a low-key event, and most people today will probably not know that it is there, but I trust it will remain on show for as long as the Cathedral stands.

Soon after I retired, Christopher also departed to set up his own investment management business and to provide a high quality investment service for wealthy individuals. It is now a most respected independent business, under his own name, and today he has a staff of some thirty people who manage £500 million of portfolios, including Mencap, a mandate he won after a Capital Radio Interview at 6.30 am!

He had been a leading light in forming a Venture Capital Fund in 1982, one of the first to be raised in London. It was called Victor Technologies, a very early desk-top computer company. Shares were bought at $2, and when floated on the market, it was growing at 25% – a month. We earned a $1,000,000 fee and that company went bust a year later.

Where have we heard all this since? 2000 was surely a copy of how dangerous it can be to gamble. One solid bit of advice is this: 'Only speculate with money you can afford to lose.' This in no way contradicts my firm belief that, over time, buying shares in top quality companies will pay handsome dividends, as will be shown later.

So, back to the beginning of my involvement and burning interest in so many differing types of charities, in which personal contact has led from one thing to another.

PART III

Work with Charities

CHAPTER ONE

Involvement with Charities

DURING THE POST-WAR YEARS most of my working time has been spent in handling pension fund monies and charitable funds as a professional, and the development of the business has grown from very small beginnings into a major financial sector not only in Great Britain, but also overseas – particularly so in the United States of America. Regular visits to the States involved talking to stockbrokers and major institutions where, in most cases, they had charitable funds. Investment of those funds was the focal point of the meetings. American statistics show that donations to charity in that country are around ten times greater per head than those in the UK. We are changing our tax rules in an endeavour to close this gap, but so far little success has been recorded, partly, I believe, because high taxation here, for so many years, militated against giving to charity, and that attitude is somewhat ingrained in people's minds. In America there have been high levels of tax relief on such donations for very many years and the citizens are more used to the habit of giving.

The work required to address this situation in Great Britain has been undertaken principally by the Charities Aid Foundation, which body was originally part of the National Council of Social Services. In 1924 the latter set up a Charities Department and in 1959 this small Fund was re-named the Charities Aid Fund. It was around 1950 that Helbert Wagg was appointed to manage the investments, which, as stated earlier, totalled around £50,000. My role was to handle what were then very few decisions that had to be made. Michael Verey and I went some three or four times a year to a very small office of only two or three rooms in Bedford Square to discuss what might be needed to be done. From those small beginnings two 'offspring' were born. One was the Social Workers Pension Fund, which Helbert Wagg was appointed to manage, and as there was then no one else in our Department, it fell to me to handle the investments. It is now very much bigger indeed and is called The Pensions Trust, worth today some £1,800,000,000 with 3,500 Charities as members. They have seven investment houses managing the investments, which include a property portfolio. The second and more major change was brought about by a new recruit to the Charities Aid Fund, namely Dick Livingston-Booth OBE, who had retired from the Colonial Service. This was in 1959 and because of his drive and energy, the Fund was, in effect, spun off from its parent body and in its independent role it was converted in 1974 into a charity in its own right and became the Charities Aid Foundation (CAF).

Because of my involvement from those small beginnings in 1950 or thereabouts, it is chronologically correct to start this section of the book by concentrating on charitable connections, many of which, as mentioned, have sprung from pension funds business.

Chapter Two

Charities Aid Foundation, 1950-2000

Today, in 2001, the staff in this great charitable business number over three hundred, and after two major moves of offices, CAF now operates from West Malling in Kent (the site of a Battle of Britain fighter station). It fills a purpose-built building of modern structure where all the 'high tec' machinery is in-house.

Its role is split into several key and separate facets, all built upon its original role of collecting covenant payments from wealthy, or not so wealthy, individuals as well as corporate bodies, whereby tax was reclaimed immediately and accounts were opened with the ensuing cash. These balances, topped up by the reclaimed tax, are all available for the donors to draw down as requested, either by standing orders or now by use of a cheque book or charity card, whereby donations can be made on a one-off basis – but payments can *only* be made to eligible charities. Although the tax rules changed in the budget of 1999, the system works in just the same way for donors who give today by means of Gift Aid rather than covenants.

On Dick Livingston-Booth's retirement in 1982, he was succeeded by Michael Brophy as Chief Executive, and he has driven CAF, the Trustees and everyone involved in a dedicated, enthusiastic and determined way ever since. He is a lateral thinker in every sense of the word and although many ideas have come to fruition, a few have not! In creating new ventures, he has had, of course, to convince not only the Trustees and senior staff, but also outside bodies, including in particular the Treasury, the Inland Revenue and the Charity Commissioners. Some of these developments have taken far too long to come to fruition, but this is what happens when Government, in its widest context, gets involved. This problem, as well as related ones, will be discussed later and any solutions that can be found, were expensive for clients, be they individuals, pension funds or charities, but what was not perhaps seen at that time was the increase in bureaucracy that would come about in order to suit the regulators, and the regulations that had to be contended with in back offices, where the paper work grew in mountains.

The likelihood of this happening was to me guaranteed, and having spent so many years in two merchant banks, it seemed an absolute certainty that *management fees* would escalate enormously, as indeed they have. This exercised my mind to a considerable extent, and with no real target in mind, I eventually wrote a forty-page document on this subject. It ventured to suggest to the then Trustees of CAF that if they launched two vehicles for charities only, they could be successful by running them on a lower-fee basis than the corporate entities in the City at large would have to charge; this was because we were a charity and did not have to make large profits, whereas commercial undertakings would *have* to make them.

This paper must have been discussed by the Trustees because the Chairman, Sir Reay Geddes KBE, sent for me and said in the end, 'You will never get away with this.' I simply said that I felt it should be pursued and left it at that. Perhaps a year or so later, we did have a meeting with others from the charity world, whose names I have forgotten. One, however, was the representative from the charity of Sainsbury's. At that meeting I was asked how large I envisaged such a vehicle becoming and, because of previous launches of new types of vehicles mentioned earlier, I replied that we should aim for £100M in five years. A vote was taken and it was agreed to go ahead. At that point Reay Geddes said, 'You have got everything you want and you have hardly said a word.' My reply was emphatic: 'Thanks for the compliment, but I have to say that I have never attended a meeting and said next to nothing.' Its growth has been well documented and I chaired both these funds virtually to retirement in March 2000, and we did reach £100m, in four years. Today they exceed £400m, with over 2,500 charities invested in each fund. It was after their launch that Reay said one day, 'We ought to pay you £5,000 a year for what you do, but we would like you to become a Trustee of CAF and you probably know that Trustees of Charities cannot be paid.'

'Let me know', he then said, and because I had just about retired from Charterhouse and knew what my pension would be, I said I would happily join the Trustees.

One further point about the two Funds is this. Each is a Charity in its own right, and as such they can both receive cash into either Fund from charities, however their Trust Deeds may have been written. Many older Trust Deeds, which are, in effect, still governed by older Trustee Investment Act rules, continue to limit the amounts of money which can be placed into equity investments, but the Balanced Growth Fund is a way of driving a coach and horses straight through the rules. It is this bit of total nonsense which has always astounded me, in that the officials have taken so long to change the rules so as to allow all charities to have freedom to invest wherever their trustees may wish. If Trustees misbehave, the law is quite clear: each Trustee is jointly and severally responsible for misdemeanours, and losses cannot be off-set against profits. As a sort of postscript, it is only from the 1st of February 2001 that Trustees are at last free to invest where they wish, subject to their own Trust Deeds in some cases. See a lawyer to make certain.

Whilst on the duties of Trustees, mention must be made of difficult decisions that have to be made by them from time to time, and in CAF there was a major debate on the question of our own investment managers. In other parts of this book, references are made to the vetting of the performance of managers, and I referred much earlier to the agonizing feelings one has when losing a business to a competitor. The stress is even greater when one finds oneself in the opposite position, namely of having to decide to replace existing managers and find a new one. For many charities this may not make headline news, but in our case it did because of the hundreds of charities that were unit holders. We did our duty, and we are totally convinced that the decision was correct, if only because the performance improved markedly.

Another new boy, elected at the same time as me to be a Trustee of CAF, was Sir Peter Baldwin, KCB, a retired Civil Servant who had been secretary to the Cabinet Office. That was another stroke of luck or an accident of timing, which led to further charitable activities at a later date. He became a superb Chairman of CAF and when both of us had done the maximum time allowed as a trustee, he became a very worthy President. I reverted to keeping a very watchful eye on the investment portfolio. During our joint time as Trustees, a great deal of progress was made in extending CAF's role in several different directions, and a very good short history of these activities was produced in 1999 in what, by modern terminology, we might well call 'bullet points.' Many of these developments were outside my role of influence, and quite right too, but when it came to overseas activities, three doors opened. First was the launch of the US operation, where virtually all of the work was done by permanent members of staff with Michael Brophy leading from the front. Because of my many visits to New York as a Merchant Banker, it was useful to have met many of the people who eventually became involved, and one such connection was quite extraordinary. The man eventually employed to leave the UK and head up the then New York effort was David Wickert, a one-time parson who had left the Church. It was his father who had really kicked PFPUT into being and so another circle was closed. That operation is still the vehicle for enabling US donations to charity (tax free, remember) to be channelled through what is now our Washington office to London and then onwards to a mass of charities world-wide.

Another vehicle was set up in Moscow to steer Government, World Bank and other moneys into the charitable sector in Russia, which then was very much in its infancy. A year on its Board of Directors was interesting in the extreme, partly because of the difficulties of breaking new ground and partly for personality reasons, which were eventually overcome. An event in which expansion did fall into my lap was the opening of offices in Sydney, Australia. Barnardo's, which comes later, have offices in that city and I knew the trustees and staff well. Better still, my daughter Nicola and her 'Brit' husband, Christopher Breach, had lived there for eighteen years and (though this had absolutely nothing to do with me) Christopher became interested when he heard about the pre-formation meetings I had had. Then to my astonishment his Bank, Macquarie Bank, sponsored its launch and Christopher is one of the first Trustees 'down under'. Good on yer, mate!

CAF now has offices to help spread charitable giving in South Africa, India, and Bulgaria. Other countries are on the target list and we have to wish them well – the need for charity is far greater than the means to supply it, so every effort must continue to be made to keep the cash flowing internationally. Perhaps the greatest proponent of this need is the current chairman of The World Bank, one Jim Wolfensohn. He was originally an Australian stockbroker in Sydney until he came to London and joined Schroders. This was where I first met him, before he went on to greater things in the United States. In his busy agenda, he squeezed in a flying visit to London and addressed a gathering of charity people in the Café Royal in 1998. I knew him well from earlier days and it was arranged that I should meet him. On entering the foyer he said, 'Good God, I thought you must be dead!' Luckily neither of us is in that permanent state, and long may he try to bring to bear greater philanthropy to those in more need than most people in the developed world can possibly visualize.

One major work which did take up a great deal of time for Trustees and staff alike was the creation of the Give as you Earn Scheme in 1987. The Charities Aid Fund invested over £3 million in the first five years to get this up and running, and to develop it into by far the most successful operation in the country. Although it will be some years before CAF breaks even in this venture, there are currently around 400,000 employees in the United Kingdom, giving in the region of £40 million per annum, tax free, to UK charities. The Scheme continues to grow strongly, and it appeals to both donors and charities in its simplicity. Donations are made by way of pre-tax deduction from pay, so donors get immediate tax relief at their marginal rates. Charities, for their part, receive a regular stream of income without the bother of having to reclaim tax. A win-win situation, and now, of course, there is no limit to the size of donations.

The further good news is that the Scheme is now in profit, and CAF is slowly being refunded for its sizeable outlay.

Commensurate with all these developments, the money still had to be husbanded and to begin closing this section, it will be worthwhile to set out some of the figures involved. More people need to know about The Charities Aid Foundation, and the role it plays in British 'giving'. It is highly cost efficient and deserves to grow at a rate far faster than it already has, but staff resources have been more than fully extended and the gratitude of recipients needs to be advertized in far more forcible ways.

A few figures today (December 2000) are as follows:

Receipts in 2000 from those using CAF donor services	£220m
Increase in 2000 of charities' funds in CAF's financial services	£160m
Total funds managed within CAF family	£1,100m
Number of donor clients	600,000
Number of charity clients	11,000
Average growth of funds managed over 5 years	23% p.a.

In spite of the amount of work, the reading and planning, all voluntary by Trustees, it has been enormously interesting and we have still been able to enjoy many lighter moments at meetings.

One of the last events I attended was a small Trustees' buffet luncheon in the Bank of England attended by some forty people who had been involved with CAF for long periods of time. Sir Edward George was most enthusiastic for our future; the Bank was one of the first corporate donors and users of CAF and they still are.

When we left the Bank of England, Michael Brophy asked me if I would like a chat and a glass of champagne opposite the Bank. It was a lovely day, and as we sat in the sun, our Chairman, Sir Brian Jenkins, asked if he could join us. I do not know how many ex-Lord Mayors of London have been seen sitting in the street imbibing a pleasant drink, but I told him what only Michael and Sir Peter Baldwin then knew. As seventy-five was looming, I had felt for some months that my role should be handed over to someone who was 'hands-on' and therefore more up-to-date with all the new rules and regulations. Those were being thrust upon the charity world by the Charity Commission and the accountancy profession, and will be touched upon later. I therefore decided to retire in March 2000 and did so.

Such is the pressure of these regulations that I am sorry to say that some Trustees are having to assess their own position from a legal point of view. From our Finance Committee, we lost two of the best brains in the City, one of whom had been a colleague at Schroders, and with whom I had kept in touch since leaving there in 1972. To have this happen is nothing short of a tragedy, when we all know how difficult it is to get good volunteers. My views on this point are well documented, and I make no apologies to anyone. Bureaucracy has gone too far and is helping to kill off the flow of those who might have considered becoming Trustees.

Brian Jenkins' response to my statement about retiring was short and to the point: 'I do not blame you.'

The calibre of those who have been Trustees over the years is perhaps best exemplified by showing, in chronological order, the names of those who have held this position, and this is lifted from the brief history noted earlier in this section.

'Throughout the 25 years CAF has had the benefit of wise and experienced Trustees who have given of their time most generously. Without their contribution this book would not be possible.'

In order of serving:-

Sir Anthony Burney OBE
Lord Allen of Abbeydale GCB
Sir Frederick Catherwood
Sir James Dunnett GCB CMG
A.C. Everett FCA
The Lord Goodman CH
W.E.A. Lewis OBE
Lady Rupert Nevill
J.K. Owens CBE
The Hon Mrs Charles Morrison
Rt Hon Lord Windlesham CVO
Nicholas Hinton CBE
Sir Alex Alexander
Peter Jay
Christopher B. Zealley
Lady Eccles DL
Kenneth Thomas

Miss Barbara Hosking OBE
William Aramaony
Sir Peter Baldwin KCB
Barrie C. Johnston OBE FPMI
Sir Harold Haywood KCVO OBE DL
Charles F. Green
Sir Geoffrey Chandler CBE
The Lady Prior
John A. Brooks CBE
Sir Richard Francis KCMG
Judy Weleminsky
Roger Lyons
Professor Naomi Sargant
The Lord Dahrendorf KBE FBA
Ian D.R. Campbell FCA
Sir Brian Jenkins GBE MA FCA
Kenneth G. Faircloth OBE BSc Econ

Dr John Treasure
Mrs Patricia Batty Shaw CBE DL
Sir John Read FCA
Sir Reay Geddes KBE
Kent de M. Price
Sir Alex Jarratt CB
Baroness Prashar CBE
William U. Jackson CBE DL
The Rt Revd Alan W Morgan,
  Bishop of Sherwood

Stuart Etherington
Sir Brian Pearse FCIB
Lady Tumim OBE
Ian Macgregor FCA
Mrs Sylvia Denman CBE
Dr J. Martin Owen FCIB PhD FCA
Sir Patrick Brown KCB
Sir Tim Chessells
Rodney Buse

and later

Roger A. Barnes
Peter Berry

Chapter Three

Royal Marines Association (c.1955 to 1999)

My reasons for getting involved with the Royal Marines Association were mentioned earlier but what was not mentioned were the Annual General Meetings, now held every September in the Commando Training Centre, Royal Marines, near Exeter. The meetings themselves are normally peaceful but occasionally a 'lower deck lawyer', either for malice, fun or genuine misunderstanding, would raise difficult questions which required eventual reference to lawyers or Chartered Accountants for them to answer. The complexity of modern accountancy rules for charities has become a nightmare for Treasurers of Charities, and small ones in particular, the degree of professionalism required to draw up accounts being difficult for most volunteers – and I am no exception. In fact many accountants have gone so far as to admit that they also find it difficult to put it into words; putting it into practice is too complicated for amateurs. To try to answer what might appear to be innocent questions when some 200 or more members are present is at times impossible. So impossible is it that in the case of our Association, and following the introduction of SORP II (Standard of Recommended Practice II), we had to pay for our auditor to attend the AGM in 1997 in Lympstone, Devon, in order to help me out. He advised me not to answer direct, to let him put it his way and, if still not clear, he would reply in writing. This story is told because, for a small charity, the cost was staggering.

In 1996, before the changes, our accountancy and audit fees were £2,988. In 1997, these charges were £6,174. and in 1998 they rose to £7,500 which included the costs of the auditors' time in attending the Annual General Meeting, As our income was some £50,000 a year,

Royal Marines Association 'standing easy'. The beginning of the Drum Head Service.

those professional fees took 15% of our income. They have now dropped back to £5,000 which is still 10%!

This has been a huge increase in costs and, more to the point, a huge cut in the amount available for charitable purposes. We knew what needed to be done, and did it at a large cost in cash and time. For some of the Trustees, who did not claim travel expenses, it was quite a burden. For instance a journey of 150 miles by car, followed by the meetings, would occupy most of a day, and usually a Saturday into the bargain. I do not believe that Trustees of many small charities have ever realized what had to be done, but the inevitability of bureaucracy will be debated later. When I was first involved with the Association, it had a very small pot of money of some £15,000 and gradually this has grown, supplemented by one very large legacy which came totally out of the blue. In 1998 we were informed by a solicitor that a Mr Clark had left the Association one third of his estate, the other two thirds of which were left to his own regimental Association, namely that of the Royal Artillery. We have tried every avenue we could think of to see what Corporal Clark's connection was with the Royal Marines, and have drawn a blank at each turn. This is one of those sad situations that arise from time to time, and it is a great pity that we cannot even thank any relative. He left our Association the sum of £160,000 and our funds today total around £1,000,000. We can only assume that a Marine must have saved his life in Normandy or somewhere else.

A fellow Trustee (or were we then just advisers?) in the early days was a retired Major, John Yates, who was a solicitor in the City of London. He had a quiet, slow and well reasoned view of what should and should not be done when setting up charities, and it was through him that we stated in our investment clause that the policy would be the same as if the assets were owned individually by the persons involved. This kept us away from the nightmare of being stuck with the old restrictive rules for investing charities' monies and we could, if we so wanted, put all the assets into ordinary shares rather than being bound by rules limiting our equity portion then to 50% of the total, with the other 50% effectively being in Gilt-Edged stocks. This has proven to have been of sizeable benefit to the Association and the problem of the 'old rules' will be mentioned later, with some degree of strength. John Yates did us all a good turn, and although sadly now long deceased, I hope he will not mind me describing him as I saw him – a real character out of Pickwick Papers. He is so sadly missed.

In common with many charities, we have, in recent years, slowly used some of our capital to balance our books; our investment philosophy has been to have most of our portfolio in ordinary shares of leading companies and some 90% is in this sector. We have thereby had sizeable increases in dividend income every year, and a small part of the capital growth has been taken out and used. The future may possibly be a little different because for some ten years we have been in a period of inflation lower than at any time since the 1950s, and this may continue for a while longer. To cope with this and all the other 'legalistic' problems, we have had to appoint a firm of professional investment portfolio managers, namely Newton Investment Management Ltd, which company continues to have a good reputation. Part of the professionalism that has crept into the charity world necessitates reviewing the performance of managers every few years – my dictat is that it *must* be looked at *every* year and that the satisfaction or otherwise of trustees has to be minuted. It is only after a trend becomes evident in a downward direction that the question of switching managers comes to the top of an agenda, and in any case, it does no harm to have a 'beauty parade' every five years to see what other fund managers are offering.

Statistics on investment management performance right across the board are readily available and Trustees of all charities need to look at these and take action if deemed necessary.

From time to time reference has been made to the strange connections that have occurred in my story so far, and they get even more frequent. One of the senior Royal Marine Officers, Col. Dick Sidwell OBE, while still serving, was an ex-officio member of the Royal Marines Association Board of Trustees, and it was through him that my appointment as a Trustee of King George's Fund for Sailors came about in 1982. This will be discussed when the topic duly arises in its chronological order. Because of meeting many of the Commandant Generals of the day, my RMA role got extended into the non-public funds of the Corps itself and then into becoming a Trustee of the Corps Museum, which was a quite different kettle of fish!

CHAPTER FOUR

Royal Marines Corps Funds

From time to time mention has been made of my high regard for serving Officers and Non-Commissioned Officers in the Royal Marines and the Royal Navy, and this sentiment is equally strong for the Army and The Royal Air Force connections, where charitable work and investment management have to some extent gone hand in hand. Successful management of the reserves of all charities will play a large part in increasing the funds that become available for the activities of charities, and this is particularly so for 'grant-giving' charities, where virtually all of the revenue will come from investments.

Many charitable organizations, such as hospitals and regimental associations, will have a dozen or more smaller pots of money which are legacies of long ago, and which are expensive to manage and audit. Indeed costs can be totally outrageous if one is trying to maintain independence when it comes to investment management fees for small amounts. There are two courses of action available to overcome these difficulties and the first of such courses is that of amalgamation, whereby the investment kitty can be put into one portfolio rather than remaining in many bits and pieces. This will reduce all the costs mentioned, but more particularly so that of investment management, because merchant banks and investment managers of all types will, understandably, be more interested in managing say £3m in one pot, rather than in managing ten pots of £300,000. Until recent times such moves have been fraught with problems with the Charity Commission, but I am happy to say that time has been of enormous help in this respect, and Trustees will now find the Charity Commission to be not only helpful, but actually keen to help. The Royal Marines funds were in this position, with individual pots for officers, for sergeants, for other ranks and even these were segregated at times into accident cases, invalid cases, other welfare efforts and so on. In our case we began amalgamating fifteen or even more years ago, and the wheels ground ever so slowly, one problem being that most such bodies have as their Trustees senior members of whatever rank the fund is aimed at, and these personnel usually retire or move on to other posts every three years or so. The reality of this has taken a long time to dawn on Trustees, and that hurdle can often be overcome when such people have private money of their own, and can therefore understand the problem. My recommendation is for such funds to have outside Trustees who can keep such plans being carried forward, and the best action of all is for the Trustees of each fund to be the same people. This will often need a Trust Deed to be altered, in which case lawyers will be needed to do the work and again, the Charity Commission will help.

In January 2001 the Corps funds were finally placed under one name and it is interesting to me that part of this process has been helped because it is not only officers who have traditionally been expected to have private money. Today all ranks have many amongst them who have inherited money from, for example, parents and grandparents. These fortunate people can make good Trustees because they really do understand what is being talked about and frequently ask managers the sort of questions that were never raised years ago. Although I take issue with some of the results of the recent Charities Acts, I have to say that the responsibility of becoming a Trustee is now far better understood by many who are asked to take on this role, and it is pleasing to record that some who cannot or do not want to take on the legal risks will frequently resign rather than be pushed!

A similar course of action concerning amalgamation has taken place for King George's Fund for Sailors, which will be discussed shortly, and which began for me in 1980.

CHAPTER FIVE

Royal Marines Museum, 1988-97

It was at one of the Corps Fund's meetings in 1988 that the then Commandant General, Lt. General Sir Martin Garrod, asked me if I had a moment to talk about something before dinner – in a corner – and his request really did take me by surprise. He said that the Ministry of Defence was planning to relieve itself of the continuing liability and responsibility of running, in every sense of the word, all the military museums that were under its wing, and that the Royal Marines were no exception. The statement from him was something along these lines: 'We are setting up a charity for this purpose and we shall probably be aiming at four serving personnel and four outside Trustees, and I would be pleased if you would agree to being one of the first such "outsiders".' Three of us had been in the Corps, so (hopefully) had a real interest in making this work, and the fourth was an admirable choice of a non ex-Marine, Nicholas (Nick) Jonas. Nick proved to have a keen interest, having military experience in the Northamphire Regiment, and later became a local director of IBM in Hampshire. He was Chairman of Hampshire County Council Development Association and a Deputy Lieutenant of Hampshire, and for these and other charitable works he was appointed OBE in 1998.

There were two very important appointment positions still to be filled apart from the Trustees, and they were the Chairman and the Director of the Museum. We then learned that the Chairman was to be Major General John Owen OBE, whom I have mentioned earlier and first met in 1975. At that time he gave me luncheon in The Honourable Artillery Company Headquarters. John, who very sadly died in 1999, was the most enthusiastic man I have ever met. He was a giant of a person in every respect, including his physical size and strength, which would be hard to match. At his memorial service he some £20,000, and later was appointed an Honorary Colonel for his services. The only case I know of a Royal Marine (or any other service man) being promoted from Lieutenant to Colonel in one move!

His Royal Highness, the Prince Philip, KG, KT, is the Captain General of our Corps, and he visited the Museum, as he had done before, to open it formally and at the luncheon he sat on each of the three tables in turn as each course changed. There were five of us on our table, and Nick Jonas said to me, 'You are going on holiday next week – where to?' 'Russia,' I said, to which he rejoined that he was too. We were both on a Swan Hellenic cruise in a small ship from Moscow to St Petersburg. I could not resist saying to Nick, 'I hope you are taking your wife – I am taking mine!' He was, and he did!! Such meetings should always be jolly occasions, and this certainly fell into that category, with considerable laughter at all tables.

Before my retiring as a Trustee, a further development was the creation of a Memorial Garden in the Museum gardens at Eastney. I have to say that in supporting this initiative of Jean's, the wife of John Owen, I really could not see it being a success and that was my second mistake. It has been a huge success, and we now have separate Memorial Plaques of each of the World War II Royal Marine Commandos, which numbered 40, 41, 42, 43, 44, 45, 46, 47 and 48. On top of that there are plaques from the Royal Marines Landing Craft Association, Post-War units and the Band Service, and other plaques, At each and every one of these a memorial service is held annually.

Jean Owen has vetted this bit for me and has written the following extract:-

> The garden, when I originally planned it, was planted in Royal Marine colours in the flower beds, the part where the anchor stands represents the sea operations of the Corps, whilst the Falklands Stone represents the land operations.

That dream of hers has undoubtedly been a smash hit.

Now comes what I think is another quite extraordinary story. At one meeting General John said he would like Trustees to visit, if possible, all the countries where the Royal Marines have served since our formation in 1664. As there are very few countries where we have not served, this was of course impossible, but we did pretty well between us. John did his best, but I suggest that the current Deputy Chairman, Tony Brend, achieved outstanding success on his round-the-world retirement trip when he was on his farewell visit to all the Commercial Union offices. He was Chief Executive of that great Company and he was responsible for raising some £40,000 in Australia, in which country was produced a very large tapestry of the famous picture of Captain Cook landing in Botany Bay. He actually volunteered to visit the Falkland Islands with me, but at the last minute he had to cry off. The purpose of the visit was to collect a sum of money raised by ex-Royal Marines who now live in the Falklands and to see if we could get a few tons of rock from the site of Mount Tumbledown, where a major part of the battle to retrieve the Islands was fought. We proposed to use this as the centrepiece for the memorial garden.

Jean Owen drew a plan of the size of stones required and I was lucky enough to ask a friend of mine who had been with me at Schroders if he would like to accompany me. He is Peter Grant, who left that company almost a year after I did when he became a director of the Cadogan Estates Company. Here a mutual colleague of Schroder days was (Lord) Charles Chelsea, now Earl Cadogan. Another strange coincidence was that Charles's first wife, who had sadly died a few years before, was a descendant of the family that had owned the land where the Museum now stands, and we are all grateful to him for the generous donation he made to our Appeal for funds.

We flew by RAF Tri-Star from Brize Norton, only some five miles from Peter's house, and after a stopover in Ascension Island, proceeded to Stanley, the capital of the Falkland Islands. The eight-day stop included visits by small aeroplane or Land Rover to most of the battle areas, including Pebble Island, Goose Green, Mount Harriet, Port Howard etc, and we were also given lunch by the then Governor, His Excellency David Tatham. At that luncheon I raised the question of the stone we required, and he agreed that that could

Falkland Islands – 'Reflection'.

be arranged but that we should have to organize transport, possibly by the Royal Navy. I also raised with him the question of a donation from the Falkland Islands Government, but sadly that failed and this continues to disappoint me. The Royal Marines National Memorial in the Mall is next to Admiralty Arch. It was re-dedicated by our Captain General, HRH Prince Philip, Duke of Edinburgh, in October 2000 and it was when reading *The Falkland Islands Journal* that I discovered that part of the £90,000 cost of its refurbishment included a generous offer from the Falkland Islands Government of £15,000 – so perhaps I did sow a small seed! On our return to the UK, the plane broke down on Ascension Island, so we had to have a stopover which in the end lasted for two days – very hot indeed! I was particularly sorry about this because I missed the memorial service to Capt. Edward Brown, CVO, DSC, RN, in a local church.

*Falkland Islands Stone – Royal Marines Museum, Memorial Garden.
With Cynthia, following the unveiling by Admiral Lord Lewin.*

He gets mentioned in the next chapter, concerned with King George's Fund for Sailors.

Soon after returning, I attended a dinner in the House of Commons and told the chap sitting next to me about my trip. He listened and then said, 'There is a man who lives at the top of your road who runs the ships that go backwards and forward with freight for the Islands – go and see him.' What an unbelievable coincidence that was! Following this up, I telephoned Mr Jepperson a day later and he said, 'Come and drink a bottle of champagne and we will talk about it.' We did – both – and Vagn Jepperson, a kindly man in his eighties, said that it would be no trouble at all and that if we got it packed properly, he would transport it back to Shoreham in one of his boats and that there would be no charge. This was such an astonishing piece of luck, it was almost unbelievable. The packages arrived safely, and he went even further. He said, 'You dig the hole and I will get one of my trucks to deliver straight into it.' I did not actually do the digging, but the Museum staff did, and the job was completed.

This generosity was totally unexpected and I still cannot believe that my neighbour at dinner should have known the very individual to whom I should speak, and even more astonishing that out of all England he should live only a couple of hundred yards away from him. It gave me much pleasure to take the Jeppersons to the Museum when the memorial was unveiled by Admiral Lord Lewin, after a short blessing by the padre, who had served in the Falkland Islands. When the small plaque was prepared to place on the stone, I made sure that Jepperson Heaton & Co had their name duly inscribed. Just as well I went to that dinner! The end of this story is that Cynthia and I took Mr and Mrs Jepperson home and he said he was taking us out to dinner locally. This he did and we had a jolly evening, marred only by the fact that for the second time in my life the waiter had put the red wine in the wrong place on the table and he knocked it down – over me and a white jacket. To our amazement the cleaners got out the stain, but fortunately it was an old jacket and needed replacing anyway. Always place wine bottles furthest from the side the waiter operates, and preferably against the wall.

The chances of all this happening must be far beyond the odds of winning the Lottery. It was very interesting and possibly the most satisfying of all my odd happenings. If I were asked to go back to the Falkland Islands, I would go like a shot. The best time of the year to go is the end of January to early February. The wild life is stunning and you can stand motionless at Volunteer Point and see the penguins walk straight past you as if you were not there.

Chapter Six

King George's Fund for Sailors, 1982-2001

THE INTRODUCTION TO THIS charity came about through a serving Colonel in the Royal Marines, Dick Sidwell OBE. He had been at our Corps Headquarters in one of his turns of duty and when occupying his particular role, he was an ex-officio Trustee of King George's Fund for Sailors. Somewhat unusually, he was later appointed a full Trustee. This Charity had been set up by King George V in 1917 as a central body for collecting funds for eventual distribution to seafarers' homes of many differing types. Its role can best be described by comparing it with the other principal Armed Services charities, namely The Army Benevolent Fund and The Royal Air Force Benevolent Fund. In these two cases, the titles speak for themselves and in cases of need disbursements are made to individuals and their families through an almonizing system. In the case of the Royal Navy, the Merchant Navy, the Royal Marines and the then Women's Royal Naval Service, all such funds which were given to KGFS were held in one name rather than having the problem of dozens of separate funds, which would have arisen had they been in the names of warships and merchant ships that had been sunk, or been badly damaged with masses of casualties.

The income from donations and successful investment management is then distributed to 'seafaring charities', which in turn look after the ageing ex-seamen in many charitable organizations up and down the country. KGFS is therefore a grant-giving charity and it currently donates, after careful scrutiny and assessment, sums of money to over one hundred such establishments every year. This outline of its purpose is, I hope, clearly set out in this brief description, and it was because of the need to have an additional Trustee who was in the investment management business that, in

1982, I was asked to have luncheon with the Chairman, Admiral Sir William O'Brien, to see whether I would be interested in joining the Trustees and, perhaps more importantly, whether the face fitted. It obviously did because the appointment was confirmed and simultaneously I joined the Investment Committee, chaired by a director of Robert Fleming & Co, David Donald. We held our committee meetings quarterly in his offices and were treated to first class luncheons afterwards, where sometimes affairs of state were continued or, if the agenda had been completed, it became a social lunch rather than a working one. Here again, luxury has gone out of the proverbial window with the changes in the need for management to make profits, and the niceties have become somewhat less with sandwiches and glasses of wine.

It was only two years later that David Donald went into hospital to have what we all thought was not a serious operation and we bade him good wishes at a lunch the previous day. It was a tremendous shock and very sad indeed to hear a day or so later that things had not gone well and that he had in fact died. It was then that I was appointed to be the Chairman of the Investment Committee, which at that time had some £10,500,000 of investments under its control. By the time of my first Annual General Meeting, always held in The Mansion House under the chairmanship for the day of The Lord Mayor of The City of London, we had £11,000,000, this increase in some six months or so being largely due to a sizeable legacy. Thus started a long and most interesting spell, ending at the Annual General Meeting in 2001, because seventy-five is the age at which Trustees have to retire, but between 1984 and 2001 a great deal has happened.

The Director General at that time was Captain Edward (Ed) Brown CVO, DSC, RN (Ret'd) and here again another extraordinary coincidence occurred. Not only did he live in Cheam, where I had spent all of my youth, but his house was virtually at the bottom of our garden and we met fairly often on the train to London. At that time many people thought that those who worked for charities should not be paid salaries at a level higher than normal rates. In fact it was expected that pay would be lower, and this particularly applied where the recipient was known to have a private income from other sources. My firm belief is that if you pay peanuts you get monkeys and the vital point here is that if you pay lower than current rates, you are either likely to be getting staff whom others would not choose to employ, or worse still, if additional demands are made, such as working longer hours for special functions, you are not likely to receive an over-enthusiastic response. It is far better to pay slightly higher wages, especially for smaller charities, where frequently only two or three people keep the operation going, because then if they are not efficient, you can replace them with those who are. Fewer staff of higher intellect are far more cost-efficient than more staff of a lower level of drive and understanding.

The person who then filled the role of what is now the Finance Director worked in the 1980s only three days a week and even then, when I needed to talk to him, he was frequently not there, because he picked and chose his days as he thought fit. It took some two or three years to adjust this situation, and for many years now we have had Finance Directors who are paid properly and who, in fact, work occasionally what might be called hours far beyond the normal call of duty.

This is certainly true of the Director General of King George's Fund for Sailors, which is now one of the tightest and most cost-efficient charities that one could wish to find. The cost of managing money has escalated in recent years because of all the regulations that have to be followed, and although this applies to all charities, it can be particularly burdensome for grant-giving charities, where all such costs are borne by them. By contrast the charities who receive grants have, in many cases, no such costs to bear. As has been mentioned before, and may well be again, the advent of 'Big Bang' in the City heralded the virtual end of 'free' advice by money managers and trustees (who still cannot be paid)). This has brought about the increased importance of measurement of investment performance by managers, in which the results are being printed, frequently in well-publicized league tables. This practice has necessitated Trustees becoming more professional and knowledgeable. What used to be a totally United Kingdom playing field for investment of monies has become a global field, where single individuals cannot possibly have a view on all currencies and all companies that are available in so many countries. To keep pace with inflation, which thankfully, in the recent period of some ten years duration, is far below what it had averaged since the end of World War II, one has to buy ordinary shares where, over long periods of years, increases in dividends have not only done that but have beaten it by a fair margin. And it is this difference over fixed interest stocks (viz Gilt-Edged securities) that has caused much debate and at times dissension amongst trustees and in very many charities. In the case of King George's Fund for Sailors, we have had, over the last twenty years anyway, some 80% of the funds in equities (mostly UK equities) and the recipient charities should be more than thankful that this has been so. Soon after taking over as Honorary Treasurer, when the FTSE 100 Index had fallen to 1277, two of the Trustees felt that they should resign. This was partly because of age, but most of all – in one case, I am certain that the cause was his constant pressing me to sell equities because the index had risen somewhat and he said it was too high! I refused and it has since risen to over 6000 and because prosperity is not going to go away, it will continue in an upward curve, albeit at times there will be blips in a downward direction, as has happened in 2000. This will be explained in greater detail in the relevant chapter on 'Inflation'.

When, in 1995, my time as Treasurer ended on reaching the age of seventy, our £11,000,000, mentioned earlier, had reached £33,000,000, with no new money being added. Today (November 2000) we have a fund of £43,000,000 in spite of the fact that in the past three years we have realized some £3,000,000 of our capital reserves to increase our giving to needy seafarers' charities. This policy cannot of course go on ad infinitum and it is constantly under review, as is the burning topic of 'how long are we all going to live?' This latter question is particularly relevant to this and other service charities, in which a large percentage of residents of homes are World War II veterans who have to be no less than about seventy-five years of age already.

The tax changes affecting dividends will have cost this charity a significant sum of money, amounting to some £200,000 a year.

The question of the ages of those who benefit from the KGFS

grants has been debated long and hard in the Finance Committee and Council for the following reasons. The longer we all live – and this is now a well-recognized fact – the more expensive it becomes to maintain those who live in homes, not only because of the ever rising costs of staff salaries, and the rising standards of property requirements, but also the additional costs of preserving good health with medicaments and possible extra nursing having to be anticipated. This problem was tackled in 1994 when we decided to ask R. Watson & Son (now Watson Wyatt), Consulting Actuaries, to research this and report thereon. There are two possible answers: one being not giving away enough to present residents and homes, therefore possibly ending up with too much money in the kitty when the 'age bulge' of World War II dies; the second being the alternative of giving away too much now, and running out of funds after, say, 2015 when any who served in World War II will necessarily be more than ninety years of age. By 2020, that bulge will surely have disappeared, and it is this balancing act which was tackled, with all the possible calculations of numbers and ages that we could muster. They included past and present members of The Royal Navy, Royal Marines, The Merchant Navy and The Women's Royal Naval Service.

This documentation is reviewed actuarially every four years, and we were early in trying to resolve the problem. In fact, we were possibly the first. Others have certainly followed, and the whole question is constantly under review. When it was initially debated, I said that I did not want to be the Honorary Treasurer who 'busted the Fund', and we have certainly not done that. The then senior partner of Watsons, John Martin, was an old acquaintance of mine through the pensions business, and it is with gratitude that we record that he gave his own time free of cost, whereas the work involved by his colleagues was quite correctly charged to us.

To finish this section, it is worth recording three wonderful social occasions that have taken place during the years with KGFS. The first was dinner on HMS *Victory* in Portsmouth Harbour, when Cynthia and I stayed the night in the Second Sea Lord's house in the Dockyard. To share in the ambience by dining in Lord Nelson's cabin is a privilege indeed, and to see the ship when there were only some

HMS Victory – King George's Fund for Sailors. Before dinner in Admiral Nelson's cabin.

Back row, l-r: Lt. Cdr. M. Cheshire (CO HMS Victory), Dr P. Watson (CEO AEA Technology), A. Bergvall (Norwegian Ship Owner), B.C. Johnston OBE (Council, KGFS), M. Hoffman (CEO Thames Water), Vice Admiral Sir Cameron Rusby, KCB, LVO (President KGFS, Scotland), Admiral Sir Michael Boyce, KCB, CBE, ADC, R. Bromley-Martin (MD Watkin), G. Hughes (MD P&O Cruises), R. Hepworth (PE International), Vice Admiral R. St.A Stephens RCN (Council, KGFS), Admiral Sir Brian Brown KCB, CBE (Chairman, KGFS), Capt. J.R.A. Norman RM (Flag Lt.)

Front row, l-r: Mrs Stephens, Mrs Watson, Mrs Bromley-Martin, Mrs Johnston, Lady Rusby, Mrs Hoffman, Mrs Hughes, Mrs Bergvall, Mrs Hepworth, Lady Brown.

*King George's Fund for Sailors. Reception at the Guildhall.
Introduction to HM The Queen.*

*King George's Fund for Sailors Reception.
Self (Hon Treasurer), HRH Prince Philip (President).*

twenty people on board is very special. A small string orchestra of four or five Royal Marines musicians played during the evening, and for me that was a bonus.

The other two occasions were functions on board The Royal Yacht, both in the Port of London. The first was hosted by Prince Andrew, when some fifty of us, including Cynthia, had a memorable dinner followed by a reception. At this stage a further one hundred or so guests came on board for cocktails and snacks. In all, I suppose we were there for some four hours, and the evening concluded with a magnificent fireworks display which we all watched from the quarter deck, the back-cloth being Tower Bridge all floodlit.

The second such event on The Royal Yacht was during its last visit to The Pool of London. It was, in reality, a farewell to a very special and splendid ship. That dinner, hosted by HRH The Prince Philip, was again as superb as one could expect, and we all had a full tour of the ship. The gangways are very narrow, and large numbers of people would be a real fire danger, but for our part, we saw just about everything, which must have been rather a rare and unusual moment. We saw the crew's quarters, the officers' quarters, the Royal Apartments (not allowed in!) and such other vital parts as the laundry and the engine room, where everything was polished to perfection. I am sure we could have had dinner off the deck!

I have, of course, kept the invitation cards and menus, which will lie in my cupboard until goodness knows when, but they make splendid souvenirs.

CHAPTER SEVEN

Barnardo's, 1980-95

OF ALL THE THINGS that have happened, I could never have expected to become part of this very large and highly efficient children's charity. It began long before 1980, when Barnardo's held a beauty parade to see which firm they thought fit to manage their portfolio of funds, comprising their reserves and their Pension Fund. Having known their Secretary, Keith Manly FCA, for some time, due to our meetings at the National Association of Pension Funds, they kindly asked if Schroders might be interested and a meeting was arranged. Several of their Trustees attended and the Schroders' team consisted of myself and a younger colleague. We won the contest and things went well up to the time when I left to join Charterhouse in 1972, and continued to go satisfactorily afterwards as well. Subsequently the Trustees split the management into two, the other house being Mercury Asset Management.

That, I thought, was the end of any connection with Barnardo's. But then I was appointed a Member of Association, which means, in a way, a sort of shareholder. The only entitlement is the ability to attend Annual General Meetings, which Barnardo's has to hold every year because it is a 'Company Limited by Guarantee'. Simply because I was interested in what went on at Barnardo's, I used to attend whenever possible. At those brief meetings one conversed with Trustees and others afterwards, and that appeared to be that! Not so it appeared, because at one of the Annual Conferences of the National Association of Pension Funds, Keith Manly said that his Council had asked him to see if I would consider becoming a Trustee. My response was an immediate: 'You must be joking', but he answered that it was far from a joke and that if I agreed, he would fix a pow-wow to take things a stage further so long as – I have said before – 'the face fitted'.

Number of Area Offices	8
Number of Staff	5,400
Number of Shops	300
Turnover per annum	£100,000,000
Number of children assisted per annum	50,000
Number of volunteers in Great Britain	250,000

Much of the work undertaken by Barnardo's is still not understood by the public. One-to-one staffing is needed for the very handicapped children, and in this respect a large slice of the work is undertaken for and on behalf of Local Authorities, who have to pay for the service which they admit they cannot handle. Local Authority funding is now 52% of the annual turnover mentioned in the table above, and now Local Authorities are being squeezed ever tighter, at the same time as revenue from investments is being savagely cut by tax changes. Ultimately, there is a limit. It is not the role of charities to subsidize governments and unless something fundamental is changed, either 'Government' will have to increase its payments, or charitable activities will have to be cut.

It is also little known that Barnardo's have had operations in New Zealand, Australia and Eire, and here again John Hillyer was in the forefront of decisions to hive them off with separate indigenous operations under their own national laws. My role in this was a minor one, as a member of the International Committee, but as I go to Australia nearly every year, the Sydney Council, staff and establishments have been very happy places to visit for a few hours, seeing at that great distance the work being continued that Dr Barnardo started so long ago.

The one safeguard that we demanded was that, should any of those activities bring our name into disrepute, we had the right to withdraw from them the use of the name 'Barnardo'.

In closing this chapter of my time, it is very sad to record that in the last twelve months, Norman Bowie and John Hillyer have both died. They did splendid work; they left a superb memory of jobs well done, and they are hard acts to follow. On the brighter side, I am deeply grateful for all the help given to me and the other Trustees by the quite outstanding staff. I wish in particular, continued success to

HRH Princess Diana signing the Visitors' Book at Chester.

Peter Hardy, whom I worked hard to see appointed as a Trustee, and who is now the Chairman of the Pension Fund, and to Andrew Stewart Roberts, an ex-colleague at Schroders, who also became a Trustee – another pleasant coincidence.

The tax changes affecting dividends have cost the Charity and the Pension Fund a total of £2,000,000, and this loss is a bitter pill to swallow and will cause an inevitable re-assessment of what can be done in the future.

One of the Trustees for part of my time was Lady Mackay, the wife of the then Lord Chancellor. She arranged for me to see Lord Mackay, because I was one of those who worked quite hard to get the Trustee Investment Acts brought up to date, and he gave me good advice on how to proceed. As mentioned before, we have still not been given 'the all clear' to invest monies, in my view, to the best advantage of charities generally. This debate has been going on for some five or six years already, in spite of pressure from so many sources. When all the statistics are so well known concerning differing avenues in which money can be invested, it really is appalling that bureaucracy cannot be short-circuited for the immediate benefit of charities and the nation. The cost of wasted time, and thus expense, is horrendous and cannot be justified. (I gather that at last, and from 1st February 2001, Trustees are now clear to invest without restriction – but remember the legal responsibilities!)

It was a great fifteen years, and those who so ably chaired Barnardo's during my time were Sir Ian Scott, Norman Bowie, Dame Gillian Wagner, Tessa Baring and Timothy Lawson. The Rev. Desmond Sherlock, who in his youth had been a 'Barnardo Boy', chaired the Executive and Finance Committee, and really had seen both sides of the Charity.

CHAPTER EIGHT

The Chartered Institute of Management Accountants, 1982-90

I AM NOT SURE WHETHER The Chartered Institute of Management Accountants should really rank as a charity, but as my involvement lasted eight years, all unpaid, it certainly was charitable from my point of view. Its timing keeps things in sequential order, in any case.

The Chairman of Charterhouse Group, then Geoffrey Rowett, had been the President of this Institution, and he obviously felt that an 'outside view' might be of help on their Finance Committee. Whether or not that proved to be the case is for others to decide, but the time flew, as it always does when one is busy. Their offices were just north of the BBC in Upper Regent Street, and the landlords were The Howard de Walden Estates. There was an opportunity which presented itself to take a lease on the property next door, also owned by The Howard de Walden Estate, and protracted negotiations took place to discuss and agree what could and could not be done to open up the dividing wall, change door positions, and install a lift etc. By yet another extraordinary coincidence, I became of use. The reason was that soon after World War II ended, a trainee joined Helbert Wagg for a year or two by the name of Count Joseph Czernin, and he was in my room for a spell of time. Thus we came to know each other fairly well. And again we were to meet because he married one of Lord Howard de Walden's daughters and we in fact managed Lord Howard de Walden's investment portfolio. I cannot possibly claim that this relationship actually did any good but it certainly did not appear to do any harm, and in tricky negotiating points it never does any harm to have friends across the table. By an even more amazing turn of chance, one other member of the Institution's Finance Committee was a member of staff at Keyser Ullman & Co Ltd, with which firm Charterhouse Japhet had amalgamated. On points of interest and practice we did not necessarily agree about investment policy, and in some respects our views were diametrically opposed, the main point of difference being that I favoured equities while he preferred fixed interest stocks. History will not, I am sure, have to decide who was right or wrong, but the Institution is still there and must be in capable hands with all the talent upon which it can call.

CHAPTER NINE

The Worshipful Company of Turners, 1983 to date

MENTION HAS BEEN MADE earlier of my long-standing colleague (Sir) Ashley Ponsonby, with whom I had many happy years of working together. One day some years before 1970 he said to me, 'You like tradition, history and pomp and circumstance – you ought to be a Liveryman.' My reply was to the point. It was, 'You do not pay me enough.'

On joining Charterhouse in 1972 one of my Board colleagues was David Shalit, a man who was heavily involved in the City hierarchy, and it was he who did get me interested. My family background, mentioned at the beginning, was that of blacksmiths, because my paternal grandfather was the son of one. We looked up the Company of Blacksmiths and the recent Master at that time was a partner of a firm of City solicitors in which my father-in-law was Senior Partner. When I contacted Phil Herring, he said that the Blacksmiths were really Sheffield orientated, and that he would submit my name to his other Company, The Turners, which was based in London. All this was at that time almost gobbledygook to me, and nothing happened for some three years or so. My enquiry had been left at the bottom of the filing, I think, but an eventual reminder got things moving. All Liverymen have to go through the process of interviews and, if chosen, their first step has to be that of becoming a Freeman of The City of London, where again a short meeting in The Guildhall results in the OK. Then you receive a small vellum stating your 'qualification' after paying a fee of, then, £10.

The step from Freeman to fully-fledged Liveryman of any Worshipful Company (there are now 101 of them) can take anything from months to several years. So what is a Livery Company and what does it do? When originally formed in the 1500s and 1600s, Livery

Companies were in essence guilds of master craftsmen in the trades of those days. They included, for example, Carpenters, Fishmongers, Mercers, Wax Chandlers, Fan Makers, Wheelwrights and so on.

The Turners are No 52 in the pecking order, and the role of Livery Companies in those days can best be described by taking our trade as an example. Our function was to protect the craft and its standards of workmanship. Gold and silver, for example, is still 'Hall Marked' (stamped with a date in the Hall of the Company) and we stamped furniture, wooden measures (pints etc.) to prove their standard, and that prevented short measures being sold. If non-stamped articles were found within the City walls, they were seized and broken up, thus reassuring customers that what they purchased was what it purported to be. Livery Companies are still being formed, and modern ones will include The Guild of Air Line Pilots, the Laundrymen, the Solicitors of the City of London and so on, where Liverymen will be practising members of their professions. For many of the older Livery Companies, the trade may well have long passed into history, and members will therefore be people who are invited to join because they are City workers, friends of existing Liverymen, people of repute and social standing etc. Those older Companies therefore have a mixed bag of professions represented by the Liverymen, and many such Companies are now largely charitable institutions and will be interested in supporting, for example, engineering, art or whatever. In the case of the Turners, when our trade was dying out, we have been accredited with being the first Livery Company to support 'excellence' by awarding scholarships and prizes in the early 1870s in annual competitions for turning. To celebrate the Millennium, we donated prizes totalling a record amount of £12,800, and grants which were gifted to charities normally supported by us in The City, The Craft, and The Company itself. We therefore have a Charitable Fund (which all new Liveries have to have when created, of £250,000) and the Lord Mayor of London always nominates his charity(ies) of the year, which all Liveries support. In the year 2000, the Lord Mayor was (Sir) Clive Martin, and by another strange coincidence, he served on Barnardo's Council for some twenty years, being there when I joined and still being there when I retired. The total raised by him for Barnardo's was £2,100,000.

Only Liverymen can elect the Lord Mayor of London, and that privilege also goes for the election of Sheriffs and election of other positions of office in the City Corporation. Long may that continue!

Each Livery will have a Court of those who have come up the batting order and who will guide the actions and activities of the Company for their time in office. Modern thinking has normally now limited the time of membership of the Court, and in our case we have to retire at the age of seventy-five, or ten years after going through the Chair as Master, whichever comes later. The senior member is the Master (normally for one year) and the differing influence of each is fascinating. In my own case my time came in 1990 and my aim was to increase our Charity Fund from a lowly £20,000 to some £200,000; it took longer than my year to achieve this, but successive Masters have worked hard to keep an upward trend, and now we have some £350,000. Part of this growth was achieved when Lloyds Bank asked us to remove three boxes from a branch which was being knocked down. We thought they had been destroyed by bombing, but we found long-lost records and artefacts, most of which sold, raising £20,000 for the Charity.

To conclude a busy year, each Master will choose some form of entertainment on the Ladies Night, as well as presenting each lady guest with a memento of the evening. In my case I had always wanted to have a Royal Marine string quartet to play during dinner, and this we did. The Commandant General and his wife were amongst my guests, and unknown to me beforehand, the Corps put on a display by five members of the Corps of Drums. My son, now also a member of the Livery, videoed this, so we have a permanent record. Different it was, and the next Master said, 'How do I follow that?' My reply was again short and to the point, 'That is your problem.' In March 2001 I came off the Court but still seem likely to have a role in looking after the money of the Company itself and the Charity – all of which has trebled in my time through successful stock market equity investing. The major credit for this goes, without any question, to a predecessor in 1946. We inherited in that year a sizeable

Worshipful Company of Turners: the Mistress and Master Turner, 1990.

legacy of some £35,000 and it all went into ordinary shares – a very far-seeing move in those days, and three Court Members resigned. None did in my time, but how similar this is to my experience at King George's Fund for Sailors.

To close this section I wonder how many people know the origin of the expression 'sixes and sevens'. It refers to two early Livery Companies which were formed on or about the same day. As no one has ever been sure of the exact timing, they take it in turn each year to be No 6 or No 7 in the pecking order. The Companies are, The Worshipful Company of Merchant Taylors and The Worshipful Company of Skinners.

There is one last, rather amusing, privilege of being a Liveryman, but I would not wish to see if it still worked. If found drunk and incapable in the streets of the City of London in the old days, the Constabulary would see that you were deposited safely on the steps of your Hall. Most Liveries today do not have a Hall!

Chapter Ten

The Spastics Society (now named SCOPE), 1984-89

MENTION HAS BEEN MADE earlier of Peter Jackson, a partner of the Accountants Hill Vellacott, where one of his many other clients was Admiral Sir John Cox, then recently retired from the Royal Navy. John had been appointed Chief Executive of The Spastics Society and through Peter a meeting was arranged to see if I might be able to help as a member of the Finance Committee. Again two coincidences occurred, the first being that Jack Wickert, who, it will be recalled, was the originator of the idea of forming The Pension Fund Property Unit Trust, was about to retire from the Finance Committee, so I knew that if he was involved, finances were under control. The second coincidence was that Don Norris, the Spastics Financial Controller, would appear later on as the Chief Accountant of The Charities' Aid Foundation, and his expertise was thus well known to me. For the first two years or so things proceeded on an even keel, but after one meeting I had a long discussion with John Cox, who told me that the way the Society had been run was causing a problem. He explained this by saying he would give his right arm for half the Council of Barnardo's, because it had such a depth of vision due to the members of Council having such a varied mixture of outside jobs and professions. This he compared with the Spastics Council, where, he said, you were only appointed to Council if you had done umpteen years of work for the Spastics Society. Hence it had a restricted understanding of problems rather than a broad outside view. I could well appreciate his problem, but it was obviously not understood by his Council. It may perhaps have been that the Council did not understand its own problem. Therefore, John Cox left the Spastics Society and on departing, he said, 'If I were you, I would resign immediately.' I told him, 'John, you got me into this role; I will stay, but should I wish to resign, I will make up my mind in my own time.' My response was the same then as it would be today in similar circumstances.

Some months later things did come to a head when I was chairing a meeting of the Spastics Society's Pension Fund Company. Those present included Noble Lowndes, a leading authority on such matters, and a new director of the Pension Fund appointed by the Society. That meeting was without doubt the worst I have ever attended anywhere, and it consisted largely of a harangue by the newly appointed director against Noble Lowndes. After half an hour or so I called a halt to the tirade, stating that in no way should experts be talked to in that manner. Furthermore, I continued, it was obvious that the director had a monumental chip on his shoulder because he had not handled his own pension affairs satisfactorily. I gave the meeting five minutes notice of my intention to leave and to submit my resignation – which I did in writing when I got home. The next day I was told that the Finance Director had also resigned, and several years later it gave me huge pleasure to see Don at the Charities' Aid Foundation where, as Chief Accountant, he has done truly superb work in what was then becoming a so much more complex world where money is concerned.

I have no doubt that time has coped with this difficulty and brought matters to a degree of order, and I trust that never again will such a situation arise in which I am involved. I have never resigned for such reasons from anything before and hope never to do so again. As a volunteer, it is possibly easier to make such a decision, but Noble Lowndes could not respond publicly, whereas I did on their behalf.

CHAPTER ELEVEN

The Imperial War Museum, 1985-87

WHEN I RETIRED FROM Charterhouse, one of their clients whose investments we managed was The Imperial War Museum, and it was my colleague Lionel Anderson who again featured in my involvement. They were about to launch an appeal to raise funds so that the establishment in Southwark could be expanded to include artefacts of all sizes, from tanks to bullets, and from midget submarines to a Spitfire. The building had been the Old Bethlem Hospital (known colloquially as Bedlam) and, long after the Great War, was in the course of being knocked down. At that point the question arose of what to do with so many objects that were decaying in an assortment of old sheds and depots up and down the country. Two wings had been knocked down and the remainder, being shaped like a flat-bottomed U, had remained so ever since. The Imperial War Museum also owns the Cabinet Rooms in Westminster, HMS *Belfast*, anchored in the Pool of London, and Duxford Airfield in Cambridgeshire, where is situated a wonderful collection of aeroplanes from all wars, including a Spitfire and Hurricane, a Lancaster Bomber, a Flying Fortress and many others.

The fund-raising was aimed purely at Lambeth and it was planned to complete the task in two years under the chairmanship of General Sir Harry Tuzo, with the Director of the Museum keeping us all on the straight and narrow. He was Dr Alan Borg, who is now the Director of the Victoria & Albert Museum and who received, in 1999, a well-earned CBE. His Deputy was Robert Crawford, and it is pleasing to be able to say that his work resulted in him taking Alan's place as the Director. He is still in office. The work entailed a large amount of paper work, which, so far as I was concerned, was carried out every Friday at the Museum for two years. In addition, I devoted to it a considerable number of hours at home, ploughing through books of solicitors, surveyors, banks, insurance companies, suppliers of arms and equipment to the services etc. Just for once, this was not purely a labour of love, because not being a trustee, I could be paid and in fact did receive a fee – not enormous, but sufficient to keep me motivated. This work was in fact quite interesting, especially when letters were sent to friends and colleagues and business connections, and even more interesting when replies were received with cheques inside the envelopes. Credit here must be given to all members of the Committee, which consisted of well known gentlemen and ladies, both military and civilian, and in my view top marks go to Alan Borg and his team. What I learned from this work has proved to be very helpful when fund-raising work was done for the Royal Marines' Museum, already mentioned, and for the Museum of The Royal Electrical and Mechanical Engineers (REME), which will be described later.

From the outside the basic structure of the Museum appears to be almost unaltered, but once inside, the difference is striking indeed. The inside walls of the U have been converted in many places so that the hollow section can be entered, leading into what is now a series of galleries which look down into a sizeable open area. Into this space have been placed some of the larger items of equipment, never previously on display. The top of this space is all glass and much of this was financed by a most generous and large donation from The Getty Foundation. In all the sum of £4,500,000 was raised publicly from both small and large donations, but on top of this, the Government donated a very welcome £12,200,000, for which the then Prime Minister, Margaret Thatcher, has to be thanked. The total raised was therefore £16,700,000. The Trustees, major donors and others were all invited to a reception at No 10 Downing Street when the work was completed, and Cynthia and I were included in the list. We naturally accepted and had a most interesting evening, being free to talk to anyone there and to see the pictures and silver etc. in some of the rooms. It is perhaps amusing to recall that when going up the famous staircase, you pass a whole line of pictures, all of past Prime Ministers, the only one in colour is that of James Callaghan. At a

CHAPTER TWELVE

Royal Navy & Royal Marines Dependent Relatives' Fund, 1985-99

THIS CHARITY IS ONE OF several in the Royal Navy, and steps are now actively being taken to amalgamate as many charities as possible in the interests of cost, in a manner similar to that mentioned earlier concerning Royal Marine funds. Charterhouse (now Newton) have managed the invested funds of this charity for many years, and on retirement I was asked to remain a member of the investment committee as an Honorary Member and in a personal capacity.

In fact, this charity differs again from what most people might think of as a 'pot of money' with income being donated to dependants. This is not the position with this Fund, which is, in effect, an insurance fund where a sum of money will be handed to the principal beneficiary within twenty-four hours of a member's death. The annual premium is very small, but the investment performance, coupled with a lower than expected death rate, has resulted in the level of payment being substantially increased. When first involved, the amount was £1,000, but this has gradually been increased, originally by some £500 a year, but more recently, by £1,000 a year, with current payments (agreed in 2000) being a meaningful £10,000.

Death of serving personnel does not have to be as a result of war, but can be from any cause, including illness or motor accident. As a precaution against a major incident, such as a jumbo jet crashing loaded, for example, with say 100 Marines or naval personnel, the Trustees have wisely taken out what can best be described as disaster insurance, which would not therefore disturb the sound footing of the Fund. As a personal comment, I must say that I doubt whether this Charity can be amalgamated with others covering different needs and which are not insurance-company structured. I shall be very interested in the outcome of this and once again my long-standing colleague and friend, Lionel Anderson, has taken my place on his retirement from Newton. For various reasons our cars almost know their own way into the Dockyard in Portsmouth.

CHAPTER THIRTEEN

SSAFA Forces Help Fund Raising Committee, 1987-88

TWO YEARS' WORK, not dissimilar to two previous fund-raising roles already mentioned, consisted largely in getting together lists of 'target' people and grant-giving charities to raise funds for a particular venture that SSAFA had in mind. This would have furthered the role that SSAFA plays in assisting ex-service personnel who might require help. This is not only by guiding applicants towards all the correct national (Government, Local Authorities etc.) bodies who must come first in such cases, but also by adding to SSAFA's own funds which can be used in the interim until the funds flow from such bodies. Their objective in forming the Committee was a good one, namely trying to reach out to all those many individuals, of all the services who should by right be seeking such assistance, but who, for whatever reason, either did not know to what they were entitled, or even if they did know, nevertheless did not apply because they might feel it was 'charity' that they would be receiving. All the services were represented, including the most senior Territorial Army Officer, Brigadier Orchard Lisle, but in the end discussions were terminated. This was partly, I believe, because the Royal British Legion felt that we were trespassing on their territory. Even then I thought that inter-service rivalry should be a thing of the past, and today, some fifteen years further down the track, I am led to believe that co-operation is very much closer. So it should be. I understand that the Royal British Legion and SSAFA Forces Help have now agreed to maintain closer co-operation in the interests of working together. It was only when writing this piece that I went to the Annual Dinner of The Old Epsomian Club and sat next to the man we were going to elect as our next President. He is Rear Admiral Ian Henderson CBE and, to my amazement, I saw on his card: 'Air Officer Commanding HQ No 3 Group RAF'. When I asked him about this seemingly odd appointment, he was very quick indeed to say that co-operation between the services was going well. And so it should be.

Another closing of the circle: the current Chairman is Lt. Gen Sir Robert Ross KCB, OBE, who has been mentioned before, and I have checked this section with him so that no false impressions can be gathered!

Chapter Fourteen

Royal Agricultural Benevolent Institution, 1987-98

YET AGAIN, ONE THING led to another, and in this case I come back to The Royal Marines, and in particular, to the Association. We have seen how senior people are, more often than not, only in positions of authority for some three, or at most four, years. In his spell of duty as The President of our Association, Peter Spurgeon had seen me in my role as The Honorary Treasurer and he had obviously taken note of my views on the investment of monies, looking in the main some four, five or many more years ahead. When Major General Peter Spurgeon CB retired from The Royal Marines, he became the Director of the Royal Agricultural Benevolent Institution, which, in a way, is yet another variation on the theme of an insurance company. It is strange to me how this type of company keeps coming my way, but it does. After one of our RM Association meetings, he said – and I can almost quote his exact words – 'I have seen you operating for the Association for a few years, would you be interested in giving the RABI a helping hand?' My response was as usual when requests like this are made, that I would like to know what the Charity did and for what purpose it had such a large pot of money, amounting in 1987 to something more than £10 million. This is an approximate figure because when my time runs out on any job of work, I always give it a year before going through what is normally a huge pile of papers. I then ruthlessly throw most of it into the paper containers in the local tip, having torn everything in half for security reasons.

RABI is a most interesting body. It was originally set up by farmers and land-owners in order to provide an income for tenant farmers who, on retirement, found themselves in a degree of financial distress. It has to be remembered that prosperity in farming has seen huge swings of fortune. Pre-World War II, it was particularly tough, with tenant farmers at times having to pay money to purchasers to get their farm (their livelihood) off their hands. After the war there was a lengthy period of prosperity with large rises in the price of good farming land. All that, at the time, was seen by the public as prosperity for all, but that was not always what it seemed. Recently we have seen some extremely tough times for farmers and land owners, and it is in changes in fortunes such as this that funds like RABI can be life-savers for many. It was in a relatively prosperous spell of time that my involvement with their finances occurred, and it was over those years, by legacies, successful investment and good management, that their reserves rose markedly to around £18,000,000 by the time of my retirement.

Some payments to recipients, rather like some Royal Navy funds already mentioned, were in the form of annuities, whereby sums of money were paid monthly to those who needed it, and again, those sums were raised from time to time to try to keep pace with the ever-increasing cost of living. To finance this, those who received money had, for much of their lives, paid what amounted to a premium annually, and those farmers knew what would come to them in due course, should misfortune occur through illness or accident which prevented them from working to normal retirement age. So far so good, but concern arose in my mind when the Trustees began thinking of expanding the numbers of those who might qualify to receive payments. What was being considered was extending the ranks of likely claimers to agricultural workers and this set alarm bells ringing in my head. I had no complaint about the thoughts and wishes – the Trustees were all farmers – but I began to take issue with what I am going to call 'back of the envelope mathematics'. Although not being an actuary (I wish I had known about that profession when at school!) I have played with numbers all my life, and was on the Boards of two small Life Assurance Companies already mentioned.

Then followed two lengthy papers by me trying to spell out the fact that they could be playing with fire; their in-house accountants, and indeed professional firms of accountants, were not the correct people to estimate the possible end-cost of such an expansion. We have witnessed, in the last two or three years, many instances of insurance companies running into enormous financial costs and trouble through mis-selling, and although in RABI's case this could not have been quite the same thing, it might have had the same outcome. It was at about this time that there was a change of personnel at the top (Peter Spurgeon had retired some years before) and his successor was aware of my concern. The employment of Consulting Actuaries in cases like this is absolutely essential – I would go further, and say imperative – whatever the cost might be. Again, you get what you pay for, and when it comes to money, as stated before, I never 'trust' anybody. What is needed in any move away from the normal is top level advice, whatever the cost, and then if things go wrong, those who gave that advice can be taken to court and damages sought. From experience this is the only course of action that should ever be taken by trustees, and especially so when, however good and honest they may be, they are non-mathematical in actuarial knowledge. One Trustee of another body, who will be mentioned later in another context, said, 'We are only doctors, you know. We know nothing about money.' When I looked at his figures I simply said, 'That is obvious,' and that is my message: if you are doctors, farmers or whatever, stick to your trade and pay properly for good advice on topics beyond your ken – cheap advice usually results in expensive experience.

To be philosophical for a moment, most of us know friends and acquaintances who have got into trouble when dealing with 'friends' and relatives and who have said loud and clear: 'there can be no trouble with this notion. I know all about the person and he will not let me down.' I repeat, when it comes to money, only trust yourself and your own judgement, but when it comes to dealing with others, get it legally drawn up and if it is money, employ the best accountants etc. that you can afford.

It was while all this was going on that it was concluded that my time had run out – it would have been interesting in the extreme to have been involved in a successful outcome to this splendid and honourable desire, and I trust that all will be well in the end.

I believe that all Boards of Trustees must have 'outsiders' appointed as Trustees, so that a broad, rather than a narrow view can be seen and understood in what is, factually, a Legal Appointment. If Trustees get things wrong by not taking proper advice, they are personally responsible for financial losses where, it has also to be understood, losses *cannot* be offset against other profits – a loss is a loss is a loss – and the responsibility is both 'joint and several'.

CHAPTER FIFTEEN

The Royal College of Radiologists, 1990-96

WHILE WORKING IN my two merchant banks, it was a pleasure and indeed a privilege to be able to assist in the management of the reserve funds of many medical establishments. These have included – in no particular order – The United Birmingham Hospitals, The Royal College of General Practitioners, already mentioned, The Royal College of Obstetricians and Gynaecologists, The Chelsea Hospital for Women, The Wright Fleming Institute of Microbiology, and others. In a way, the Trustees of these most worthy establishments fit in with comments made in the last section, in that the individuals were almost wholly medical men. While some had a knowledge of money and money matters, others emphatically did not. Perhaps my oldest (in time) City connection was one Ted Goodacre, a partner in a now extinct, but then well-known, stockbroking firm by the name of Robert Wigram & Co. It was through Ted that the introduction to the Radiologists came about. I keep coming back to the odd coincidences in life, and they are not yet finished, but Ted and I both live in Ewell, Surrey, albeit at almost the opposite ends of what is still largely a village.

One day he telephoned to ask whether I would consider helping a friend of his, a certain Dr Oscar Craig, the then President of the Royal College of Radiologists, as he wished to discuss with someone his College's financial state of affairs. Then came an even more odd coincidence: Oscar lived (and still does) in a house in Cheam, where certainly half of my life has been spent, and I would have passed by his house literally thousands upon thousands of times to and from the station every day for twenty years and more. We duly met, and it was Oscar who, as described in the last section, said, 'We are only doctors, you know, and we do not know about money'. That was a statement of the obvious, and so began six years of very regular meetings at their Headquarters. They are in the fortunate position of owning the freehold of splendid offices almost next door to the BBC, but further north, up Portland Place. They had been the recipients of several legacies, but one in particular was large by any standards and for a while capital expenditure plus commensurate costs had escalated. So much had they escalated that when I came into the picture, the income and expenditure account was well into the red. They were 100% correct in seeking professional advice, and although I was voluntary, there was a lawyer and an accountant also on the Finance Committee. Together we are, I think, justified in saying that between us we did a pretty good job in putting affairs very much on the straight and narrow in a relatively short space of time. To be equally accurate and fair, I give the doctors top marks for not only listening to what we said to them, but for biting the bullet quickly and effectively. It is no good listening to professional advice, and paying for it when necessary, and then not doing anything about it. They did, and things are now as they should be. I retired from that Committee in 1996 because not only were the finances as they should be, but – and I understand this – they held many meetings on Friday evenings. Some committee members travelled from the north of England when their week's work was ended, whereas I was now mostly at home on Fridays and did not wish to be missing from family life and Cynthia's cooking more than needs be!

My last official function with the Royal College was at their Annual Dinner, when Cynthia joined me (before our marriage she had been a radiographer) and part of that evening was spent in talking to medical men and ladies. She was more at home with that than was I, but when the speech-making took place, the then President, Dr Michael Brindle, went through the principal guests saying a few well judged words about each in turn until he came to me. In the first place I was never anticipating that my name would ever be mentioned, and when he started on me I was therefore not only astonished bur somewhat apprehensive about what he would say. Gratitude certainly was mentioned, and then came one of the most unexpected and pleasant surprises I have ever had. Dr Brindle said –

The Royal College of Radiologists. Honorary Fellowship, 1996, with the President, Dr Michael Brindle.

and I think I quote him accurately – 'The Council of the Royal College this afternoon resolved unanimously that Barrie Johnston be elected an Honorary Fellow.' They had kept that secret, and no one had even hinted beforehand what was about to be said. I now have a huge certificate on my study wall to this effect, stating at the bottom, 'This Certificate does not entitle the holder to practise!' Quite right too, and the nearest I shall ever get to being a doctor – perhaps I should have paid more attention when at Epsom College, the starting place for so very many doctors, surgeons and other medical people. It will be recalled that my first head of house became the President of the Royal College of Surgeons, Sir Alan Parks.

Although Oscar will not receive another mention, my gratitude to him is enormous and I do wear the excellent tie. However, his wife, Nancy, does come into the picture shortly, and here again another unconnected episode occurs. What they actually said to me was: 'put it on your visiting card.' 'Why?' said I. 'Because if you get took sick and collapse in the street or something worse, you will get looked after.' It is on my cards, but I am not intending to see if it will work!

CHAPTER SIXTEEN

The Ralph Snow Charity, 1992-99 including The Croydon Almshouse & Relief in Need Charities, 1968-72 & 1978-84

THE CONNECTION with the Croydon Charities (of which the Almshouse Charity of Elis David was formed over 550 years ago) goes back many years, again to Peter Jackson, who, it will be recalled, became my accountant. The management of their funds was won when still at Schroders, but it later followed me to Charterhouse, where my ex-colleagues (now at Newton following the amalgamation) still handle the portfolio. Most sadly, Peter Jackson died at a relatively young age and thus my personal connection was broken, but on my retirement I was asked to fill the role of Independent Investment Consultant to the Ralph Snow Trustees and this continued for seven years.

The Ralph Snow Charity was originally created under his 1707 Will by Ralph Snow. The administration of this and the Croydon Charities is provided in the person of Bill Rymer, a partner in the firm of Croydon solicitors, Streeter Marshall.

The founder of the Almshouses would certainly be pleased and proud to see how his generosity has prospered for the benefit of those who are fortunate enough to live there. In addition, the Relief in Need Charities has been able to provide grants to local organizations and individuals in Croydon which have benefited many.

It had been in 1992 that the Snow Charity received a significant sum from a property it owns abutting the Whitgift Centre in Croydon, and which became available for investment in the stock market. The income is divisible partially for educational purposes, and partially for another almshouse just outside Canterbury, and therefore, again over the years, many have benefited, both the young and the elderly.

The statutory restrictions on investment facing trustees have limited total freedom of where money can be invested. There have been far too many years of vacillation, caused by political timetable problems and changes of Government. Thankfully, things are now at last slowly improving. The cost to all charities limited by the old Act is considerable indeed, and this will be a subject for discussion later.

Cynthia and I were invited to see 'once more' if the face fitted. And so began in 1993 what still is for me yet another interesting spell of years and dramatic growth. There is a vast difference between running a small charity and a large one. In the former case, there are very small numbers of staff and they have to do everything between them, from planning to making the tea. In our case, we have been extraordinarily lucky to have staff who have been able to do this, and, as we shall see shortly, much more besides. In the case of larger charities, there will be specialist staff to cover, for example, accountancy, the law, staff relations, pension expertise and so on. When I arrived on the scene, I think it is fair to say that Hearing Dogs for Deaf People was at the cross-roads of having to make the leap from small to big. Sadly, in a way, things then have to become much more formal. Controls have to be inserted in systems which themselves have had to be built virtually from nothing. Meetings have to be tighter in terms of agendas, minutes and follow-ups from meetings, and above all, the actual legal responsibility of Trustees has become a reality rather than something which, perhaps, was never even considered in the early days. To sum up this small piece of philosophical debate, these changes sometimes need different people and that can be painful, but it is to the credit of our staff that they have been able to cope with all this, leaving the Trustees sleeping easy in the knowledge that all is under control. Expertise has been added to the body of Trustees, and donors and sponsors can also be sure that money is not wasted.

So, from 1993 to date, what has happened to keep everyone flat out in work? We have raised money, planned for expansion, bought two new properties, more than doubled our output of dog training, more than doubled the number of dogs living with the deaf people, and more than doubled the number of staff. A few words about each of these will I hope complete the picture.

Money

On first becoming involved, I was smitten with the emotive topic of dogs helping people and the fact that this was likely to be a magnet for legacies and donations. Our mission is, and I quote:-

'This growing Charity is dedicated to improve the quality of life of deaf people by supplying them with dogs trained to alert them to chosen everyday sounds.

We have three main objectives:
1. To select and train dogs for specific recipients and thereafter monitor their welfare.
2. To maintain and expand our training facilities, and
3. To maintain and develop a strong fund-raising capability.

We aim to increase the number of trained dogs so that more people can enjoy greater independence, confidence and security as well as the blessing of companionship.'

A lady in Banstead, the next village to us at home, was shopping, as were we, when Cynthia said, 'Look – that dog has got a Hearing Dog coat on its back'. We spoke to the lady and I said I was on the Council of Hearing Dogs. Straightaway she replied, 'You have changed my life – people stop and communicate with me whereas before I had one of your dogs I was cut off from the world.' That explains in plain English precisely what we are doing for the profoundly deaf, and that message inspires people to donate money to us and/or leave us a legacy in their Wills. We can have no better fund raisers than our dogs themselves, which come in all shapes and sizes.

The increase in cash flow, in spite of large commitments for capital expenditure, has resulted in us having funds available for investment, thus producing more income. To start with we placed spare cash in both the Income and Growth Funds of the Charities Aid Foundation, but as we began to inherit stocks and shares, we appointed Quilter & Co to manage the resultant portfolio, which increases regularly with further legacies. All future capital requirements are calculated to the penny, and cash for those plans is kept in short-term deposits, thus being free from price movements in stock markets.

Property
The site in Lewknor, Oxfordshire, cannot be further extended, so in order to expand our capacity to train dogs, we purchased a second site in Yorkshire which has been adapted to suit our purposes. The cost of both sites has been paid off, as have the development and

improvement costs. All this is shown in our balance sheet and currently it amounts to over £4,000,000 before depreciation, with another £1,500,000 to be added over the next year or two.

By keeping our eyes and ears wide open in 1996, we learnt that a wonderful small farm with four cottages, known as Grange Farm, was coming on to the market, and after lengthy discussions with planning authorities and all the other regulatory bodies, we purchased twenty-seven acres of paddocks, a fine scheduled house and many barns and old buildings. Some of these have already been knocked down, rebuilt and extended. The site itself is far enough from any other houses to be well out of earshot of barking dogs. The first stage was formally opened in 1999 by the Lord Lieutenant of Oxfordshire, Sir Nigel Mobbs, who is yet another contact and friend – he was the Chairman of Charterhouse Group for some of my time there, and he was Master of The Worshipful Company of Spectacle Makers when I was Master Turner. Again, it is always helpful to have a friend at Court! Every bit of publicity is a bonus as well.

Our Dogs
Unlike Guide Dogs for the Blind, where largish animals are essential, we can and do find dogs of all sizes and shapes, and mongrels as well as those with pedigrees. We do not pay for dogs. We get them mainly from rescue centres, dog pounds and veterinary practices, and also from individuals who, for whatever reason, need to part company with their pets. The younger these are, the better.

All dogs offered to us are tested for adaptability, health and general suitability, and after a period of socialization of between four and nine months in the home of a volunteer under the supervision of the charity, are matched with a deaf applicant. They then begin their four months' intensive training at one of the centres. The applicant is then invited to the centre to meet the dog before returning for a residential week, during which they are taught how to care for the dog and to respond to its training. A skilled trainer then spends the following week with the deaf recipient working in their home, so as to ensure that the dog has transferred its training to its new environment and has started to bond with its new owner. We never let the dogs out of our control – they are visited annually to ensure that all is well and that the dogs are in good health, working correctly and are happy in their homes. We now have 750 dogs with recipients. What, then, you are probably now asking yourselves, do these dogs do?

They are trained to differentiate between a front door bell, a back door knock, a telephone, a cooker timer, an alarm clock, a baby crying and a smoke alarm. On hearing any one of these sounds the dogs will find their owner, touch him or her with a paw, and then lead them to the source of the sound. For waking the owner up in the morning they will run up the stairs and jump on his or her bed. Some of you may well wonder what is the good of a telephone for a deaf person. There is equipment to amplify sound (which in some cases is of great value) and for others text phones are now available and this really does reduce the feeling of being cut off from society. Apart from all this, the owner gets exercise when walking the dog and, perhaps above all, the pet is company at all times of the day and during long evenings.

Our Staff at Hearing Dogs for Deaf People
The staff are split into various categories and include dog trainers, kennel staff, those who visit our dogs around the country, administrative, fund-raising, public relations and accounting personnel. All have steadily increased with the demand for the hearing dog and now number eighty. When The Grange is fully working, the number will increase to around 100.

Its great advantage is that we also own the four cottages, two on each side of the entrance to the site of Grange Farm, and these are used to house staff, for which they have to pay a fair rent. The security of the farm is therefore as sure as we can make it, aided, as is normal these days, by closed circuit television. There is an increasing number of branches in the country, where the number of volunteers is also rising. To handle communication with these hard-working men and women is a major task, coupled as it is with advice that needs to be given to those enthusiasts who are forming the new branches so essential for fund-raising in the highly competitive times in which we live. The administrative staff is therefore also increasing, but the team is small in number and very hard-working. It is because of this expansion, and the relative isolation of our properties, that we have to provide living accommodation for staff. The purchase of Grange Farm was an extraordinary chance, and the grabbing of it with both hands has more than justified the action taken for all these reasons, as well as for the fact that it was timely, with a price that would be much higher today. We cannot praise enough the energy and enterprise of Tony Blunt in seeing so much work, new to him and to us, to satisfactory completion.

It is real pleasure to be able to record that he was awarded an MBE in the Honours List of June 2001 – there can be no more worthy a recipient.

Chapter Eighteen

Honour, 1994

Some two years before 1994, the Royal Marines Headquarters staff asked if I had an up-to-date Curriculum Vitae (CV), and if so, could they have one. As so many people have asked at times for a copy to be circulated to trustees of charities, where they thought there might be mutual interest in helping them, I always had a copy at hand, which needed only a little addition or subtraction from the list of activities when such a request was made. Being inquisitive by nature, I asked them why they wanted one, and the reply was, 'We are going to try to get you something for all the years of work that you have done for us.' That was another one of those few occasions that left me somewhat short of words, because such a thing had never crossed my mind. They received the CV and that was that for some months. In fact after a year I thought that it had almost certainly been filed, but I was told by them that a second shot was going to be fired off. Again six months or so went by and nothing happened, so that I really shut it out of my mind. On 15th November 1993 a letter came through the letter box with 'Prime Minister' on it, and that sent the pulse racing a bit.

The wording always amuses me, and others in a similar position I expect, because the letter states: 'the Prime Minister has it in mind to submit your name to the Queen for an honour (or words to that effect), and that an OBE is offered.' Bearing in mind that one is not supposed to tell anyone about this, I even refrained from telling Cynthia for a couple of weeks. I ought to have known better really, because she is a genius at keeping secrets and for twenty-five years I never knew anything about what she did at the Citizens Advice Bureau where she had worked for two full days a week, in addition to training courses. That letter also states that no further communication will take place, but that it will be in the newspapers on whatever

Chapter Nineteen

VE Day Celebrations, 6th & 7th May 1995

Being Honorary Treasurer of King George's Fund for Sailors, I was aware that I would receive an invitation to attend the celebratory events for VE Day, but at that moment I did not know what was to happen. All I did was to arrange for the letter of invitation to go direct to KGFS, because I was going to Australia with Cynthia to stay with our daughter, Nicola, and family in Sydney; the Charity, I felt, could answer the invitation positively. We returned on 24th April and during that day the telephone rang and a Colonel (name forgotten) said, 'Are you coming to the events?' The letter had not been opened as it should have been, so I apologized and said, 'Yes, please.'

'Are you coming to the luncheon, Sir?'

'Where does it take place?' I asked. 'Buckingham Palace, Sir,' he replied. I could not believe my ears. 'You must be joking,' I exclaimed.

'We do not joke about that sort of thing, Mr Johnston'. 'Are you sure you have the right Johnston?' I asked.

'Absolutely, Sir,' so I went through perhaps the most amazing couple of days that anyone could ever wish to have anywhere. That was on Saturday 6th May 1995, followed by Sunday 7th May 1995.

On the Saturday evening, the celebrations began with the banquet in the Guildhall in the City of London, where I seem to remember there were some forty Heads of State present, and sitting next to our Queen was the King of Jordan. The seating plan must have taken weeks to work out, for there were some 500 people present (I did not count all on the list), and the interesting point about that outstanding dinner was that the speeches took place before the meal. If I am wrong about the reason for this, I apologize, but I was told that as this part was being televised, it had to go out on the air before the Lottery Draw! In any case, this arrangement is to be recommended because the speeches are short and one is very attentive. Post-dinner speeches can be far too long and pompous, as we all know, and when hot food is prepared, the first system does ensure that there is a time limit which is not ignored.

The menu was on silk, with edging of gold wire, and we were presented with this in a long red box, rather like a case for a Field Marshal's baton – I am sure we all felt like one anyway!

The next day saw many of us in St Paul's Cathedral for the celebratory service, and, as one would expect, the organization was faultless. I was given a pass to park my car in The Mall and instructed to board a coach to take us to St Paul's, and I for one only had one cup of tea for my early breakfast! Surprise upon surprise, when we boarded the coach, there were two holders of the Victoria Cross, two or three High Commissioners, James Callaghan, Paddy Ashdown and a few others. At St Paul's we were separately conducted to our seats (some seven rows behind the Royal Party in my case) and when the service was over, each one of us was escorted into line behind the VIP contingent. Then we proceeded down the aisle and boarded the coach, to be driven, with police escort, direct to Buckingham Palace for lunch. That was an amazing privilege because, apart from the Royal family and other VIP guests from the Government and the Household, there were only some twenty-four people from other organizations. On my table were the Treasurers of the Army Benevolent Fund, the RAF Benevolent Fund and others in equivalent roles, chaired by Sir Robert Fellowes, the Private Secretary to the Queen.

What must go on behind the scenes in organizing such an event is mind-boggling. I think they chose guests for this part of the function from those who had WW II medals, because even Admirals of post-war vintage lunched elsewhere. That has really given me a laugh from time to time, but wherever we lunched, it was a truly unbelievable day, followed, in scorching weather, by the Hyde Park parade. Walking back to our cars was a memorable event in itself. People with medals did not take them off; many people ran down

Park Lane with huge Union Flags blowing in the wind, and cars and taxis were frequently seen with flags tied to their aerials. There is still pride in our country and long may that be a reality, should – heaven forbid – another 'call to arms' be made on the next generation(s).

CHAPTER TWENTY

The Royal Association for Disability & Rehabilitation (RADAR), 1985-98

As with Hearing Dogs for Deaf People, it was Sir Peter Baldwin who involved me with RADAR, a charity which had previously been no more than a name to me. Since we were meeting regularly in the Committees of the Charities Aid Foundation (of which he was Chairman from 1994 to 1998 and subsequently President), neither of us can be surprised that we became interested in the numerous different charities which were taking much of our attention.

RADAR stands for the Royal Association for Disability and Rehabilitation. Sir Peter had come across it through his concern, as Permanent Secretary of the Department of Transport, with trying to find ways to end the exclusion of people with disabilities from the mobility which 88% of us enjoy in Britain. In addition to Shank's pony and bicycles, our mobility comes via cars, taxis, buses, coaches, trams, railways, by ships or ferries, or by aircraft. Each mechanical mode has to be made to operate with ready access to vehicles and with an infrastructure, down to the mere pavement, providing unobstructed access to it, whatever the disability one may have. This revolution, unfinished as yet, is the work of a remarkably small group of understanding and tenacious people, including disabled people, in government (and opposition), local authorities, the transport industries, the vehicle manufacturers, charities, lobbies and the media. It has spread world-wide, owing a great deal in that respect to the impetus given by the dedication of 1981 as the International Year of Disabled People and to subsequent international conferences.

As 1981 was approaching, Sir Peter's Department had looked for an organization which could speak in a representative way for disabled people of any age in order to ensure that any measure which was conceived to provide mobility would work with the grain of disabled people's lives. RADAR exactly filled this need, as a registered charity in its own right concerned with the welfare of anyone with any disability. RADAR was also providing, as it still does, the expert secretariat for the All Party Disablement Group of the two Houses of Parliament. It has its own membership, comprising more than 200 charities with particular concerns in the field of disability, together with more than as many again drawn from local authorities, service providers, suppliers, and even individual disabled people. From this membership it continually draws first-hand understanding of disabled people's needs and in the same arena it can test opinion on proposed initiatives. In order to articulate its advocacy in terms of practicable action, it engages and trains staff as experts in the law and practice in particular fields of public policy. In order to ensure that the Charity operates with full understanding of the circumstances of life for disabled people, the Charity's rules require that at least half (in practice even 90%) of the members of the Executive Committee are people who themselves have a disability; and in effect, that the chief executive of the Charity will also be a disabled person.

An institutional link between a Government Department and this Charity would have been important enough for Sir Peter's purpose at the beginning of the 1980s. But the link proved to be much more productive because, on the one hand, he had the advantage of being able to entrust the role of leadership of the Department to an exceptional civil servant (who was, and still is, also involved personally in another charity, for disabled and able-bodied children alike), Ann Frye OBE; and, on the other hand, RADAR was able to deploy the equally exceptional Bert Massie, who from infancy had been physically disabled by polio. On retiring from the Department in 1982, Sir Peter became a member of RADAR's Executive Committee. From 1986 to 1992 he also served as the first Chairman of the statutory Disabled Persons Advisory Committee, of which Bert Massie was a member, and with which Ann Frye is her Minister's link. By 1990 Bert Massie had become the Director of RADAR and by 1992 Sir Peter had become Chairman of RADAR's Executive Committee.

Together in this association for four years, Sir Peter and Bert Massie confronted the task of trying to match disabled people's needs, as children or adults, in an ever changing social and legislative scene, for advice and support in education, employment, housing mobility, social security, health, recreation, entertainment and sport. Disabled people, unfortunately, often enter these fields in the face of discrimination which, though usually inadvertent, can massively impede their access to the service or facility which they need, or even to mere opportunity. This wide range of activity has required RADAR to maintain a staff of between thirty and forty full-time salaried staff, including a group specializing in Parliamentary business.

One of RADAR's greatest successes relates to persuasion of Administrations and politicians to amend proposals in, for example, the eligibility of the disabled for benefits totalling many millions of pounds. In order not to cross wires, RADAR's voice in appealing for donations to sustain its role is muted, and its fund-raising task consequently the harder. Sir Peter was the more anxious to make every penny count in RADAR's management of its money. That is why in 1995 he asked me to have a look at RADAR with him.

I found a Charity with a demanding mission which, since its inception in comprehensive form in 1972, has been recognized by HM The Queen Mother, who has graced it without intermission as its Patron. The terms of that mission are these:

'RADAR promotes the equality of rights and obligations throughout society. It works to enable people with any disability to control their own lives and enjoy to the full the opportunities which society, the economy and the environment provide.'

The Charity's agenda is formidable:

'To care for, relieve, rehabilitate and generally assist disabled people and to promote understanding of the treatment of disability and fuller knowledge of the causes of disablement and understanding of the ways in which such causes may be eliminated or reduced.

'To promote the education, welfare and rehabilitation of disabled people and their integration within the community.

'To promote and support research into the causes, prevention, receipts from their nadir of £173,801 in 1994-95 to £458,273 in 1995-96 and £529,715 in 1996-97. The total then fluctuated between 1997-98 and 1998-99, down to £286,526 and back up as far as £359,638.

Against this background of difficulty and effort in sustaining the calls for RADAR's services, it is not surprising that Sir Peter invited me in 1995 to see whether money could be set aside in investments and be made to work successfully for capital growth and an increasing flow of income.

When I began to look into the possibilities, I found that RADAR's Honorary Treasurer at the time, Ian Eiloart, a retired chartered accountant, was giving, with much travelling, meticulous professional attention to the way in which the Charity's funds were being deployed. He had used the steady receipts in donations and grants of 1993-94, with careful budgeting, to build the aggregate of investments of general and restricted funds from £116,304 to £355,305, producing a rate of annual return of some £25,000. After some reflection I decided to propose, as has been mentioned in relation to other charities, that the services of Quilter's, and more particularly of Charles Maisey of that firm, should be engaged as brokers for the Charity. The Executive Committee accepted this suggestion and the results proved to be very much to their advantage and to Charles Maisey's credit. In 1996-97 the aggregate value of the investments rose to £512,701 and the annual income to £47,631. In the following year, 1997-98, while the annual return fell back to £34,912, the aggregate value of the investments rose to £609,855.

But the situation was to change. Sir Peter had retired from RADAR's Chair in 1996 but carried on in the Chair of its fund-raising Committee until 1999. Ian Eiloart retired from the office of Honorary Treasurer and membership of the Executive Committee in 1999. I had retired in 1998 because the finances were in good shape and I had done my job. After the General Election of 1997 Bert Massie was pressed by Ministers of the new Administration to accept the Chair of the Disability Discrimination Commission. He eventually did so in 1999.

Unfortunately, 1999-2000 proved to be a year in which the total of donations received in the year fell by £129,228, project grants fell by

£200,084 (and unrestricted grant did not rise); and the Trading Company's surplus on the year fell by £173,211, partly at least because of changed conditions in the market. This abrupt fall of £502,523 in gross annual receipts presented a problem in maintaining the Charity's reserves at the level which would avoid insolvency. A number of redundancies were declared and the Charity's programmes of work were reduced in range. The growth which had been achieved in investments took part of the strain and the reserves proved sufficient while a fresh strategy was devised and implemented to restore the Charity's capacity.

Fortunately, a happy agreement evolved between RADAR and one of the charities in membership with it, the Enham Trust. This Trust had a long and honourable record – to my personal knowledge – of providing, in the El Alamein Village in Hampshire, residential and training services, originally for members of HM Armed Forces injured in action, but now for disabled people generally. It had reached the stage where financially and philosophically it could aspire to exercise its influence for disabled people nationally. Association directly with RADAR would provide the networks already in place to enable it to do so if the Trust were to provide financial security for maintaining and further developing those networks. Conversely, RADAR, having successfully set about involving itself through its trading company in using its expertise as a source of earnings, would find assurance in association with a charity accustomed to earning income from expert services.

Finding so much to admire in these two charities' records, I am pleased by the prospect of their performance together in the interests of disabled people.

CHAPTER TWENTY-ONE

The British Federation of Women Graduates Charitable Foundation, 1995-98

APART FROM HAVING roles in managing reserve funds of so many differing charities in my working days in the City of London, involvement in hands-on roles, either as a trustee or Consultant, had never even crossed my mind before about 1980, when this course of events really began with Barnardo's. One thing has always led to another in so many differing directions, and the Livery Companies became a further avenue, this time into the finances of an academic body where all the Trustees were ladies with considerable university experience.

When one finishes the year in office as Master of a Livery Company, there is often one amongst those 101 Companies who wishes to keep the connection and friendship of that year for a while longer, and the '1990 Vintage' was no exception. The usual format is a low-key luncheon once a year, and possibly an evening dinner with one's partner. Ours has been kept in existence for ten years. It is currently run by Roger Griffiths, the Past Master of The Worshipful Company of Wax Chandlers.

At one of these lunches, in 1995, sitting next to Adrian Watney, the Past Master of the Worshipful Company of Mercers, the conversation drifted into that of the charitable world where he was a Trustee (Governor) of the industrious body of ladies mentioned in the title. They had a fairly large fund of investments, from which the income was partially used to keep in existence a very small office in a building they owned in London. Some of the rooms on the upper floors were let to tenants. The Secretary was to some extent part time, but there was one person who kept the charity ticking over and who was in the office every day and worked, in my view, very hard indeed. It was another case of 'if there is work to be done, you go home late', and the devotion to duty in this case needed a better salary. This truly was one of those cases where we would have been 'up the creek without a paddle' if she had left, and when my time to retire was approaching, my successor and I really did push the point very firmly that this had to be corrected. It was, with a planned progression in salary covering the next three years or so.

The work of the charity was that of giving grants to university graduates from around the world who wished to do research work in Britain for limited spells of time – a few weeks to a few months. The successful applicants received relatively small sums of money to aid them in maintenance including rent and food bills. By a quite strange coincidence, many years previously, the charity had been given a meaningful legacy by a Miss Sybil Campbell, one of the daughters of a director of Helbert Wagg & Co, where I started work in 1941. Writing this piece has reminded me of a few words of wisdom that I received when managing part of that family's investments so many years ago. 'Do not leave money to children when they reach twenty-one years of age; leave it to them at thirty years of age.' From a professional point of view, this is a real truism – so often twenty-one-year-olds will 'blue' that money, from lack of experience or whatever, but at thirty there is usually wisdom and an understanding of the value of money. In the case of the Campbell sisters, that was certainly true, and it was because of that that Cynthia and I had the same arrangement in our wills for our children. I told them this when they were sixteen, and they thought that thirty seemed an eternity away, but both are now over the mid-forties, so luckily for us and them, that age limit was not needed – they are still waiting, thank goodness!

My mother-in law, who, it will be recalled, lived next door and was a lovely lady, once said to me, 'You will have a long wait for my money' – she was just on ninety when she sadly died, but her investments, all in equities, were worth the waiting!

Chapter Twenty-Two

The Royal Electrical & Mechanical Engineers (REME), 1999 to date

THE WORSHIPFUL COMPANY OF TURNERS, four hundred years old in 2004, is, as you may recall, heavily involved in engineering-type grants to young men and women who are studying for qualifications, both in the Services and in civilian life. The Turners are particularly close to REME, which regiment was founded in 1942, and many of its officers have become Liverymen because of this connection. The current Master, Major General Christopher Tyler CB, was one of these, as was his father, Major General Sir Leslie Tyler KCB, the first Commandant of this Corps, then the largest in the British Army. Because of amalgamations, the Royal Logistics Corps has since taken first place, but REME remains No 1 in the technical category.

At one of our formal guest nights, our Clerk, who draws up the seating plan, sat me next to REME's Major General Besgrove CBE. In conversation he happened to say something about their Museum which they were wishing to expand, and told me that they were going through ideas for fund-raising. In response, I gave him a few points to consider, and he asked how I had been involved in such schemes. Two years' planning for fund-raising for the Imperial War Museum and eight years as a Trustee of the Royal Marines Museum – that must have satisfied him that what I had said was not totally irrelevant, because he asked if I could find time to visit their Regimental Headquarters in Arborfield, near Reading, to talk things over. After the initial introduction to others, some of whose names I struggle to recall, we had a good working luncheon, following which I was asked if I would agree to join a small working party to 'to kick the ball along'.

In two years we have gone a long way in fund-raising, building and planning for the future. There is a recognized need to gather many old artefacts into one place, where they can be visible to the public rather than hidden away in multifarious sheds and hangars up and down the country. Virtually none of these have air and temperature control to preserve their treasures, and all of such places are 'behind bars' to the public. With the rationalization that is going on in the Services, it is well understood that if left too late, some of British Army history may well be lost for all time. Thus there is an urgency to get on with the job. This is very much a case of *déjà vu*, when one looks back at the history of The Imperial War Museum and many other similar institutions.

REME also has unique large vehicles and artefacts of all shapes and sizes, many now being of considerable age. Those include tanks and battle control wagons, some having been built before World War II. The preservation of such items is labour intensive, needing highly skilled personnel to do the work of reconstruction, much of which is also 'voluntary'.

The relationship between REME and the Royal Marines is also very close. REME personnel, for example, carry out the electrical work on much of the RM equipment, as was well documented after the Falklands War. It is also close for another reason, which is that the Commanding Officer of The Commando Logistic Regiment used to alternate between the two regiments as each retired from his term of duty, so personnel at all levels are used to co-operating. The Commando Logistic Regiment is now solely under the command of RM personnel. This friendship proved to be helpful in another way. The REME senior team in charge of their Museum spent a day with me in The Royal Marine Museum in Eastney, during which ideas were exchanged quite freely, and I know the REME team appreciated the advice they received.

One of the best bits of advice that can be given when putting together teams to form committees, is to have a breadth of knowledge and business acumen, and as mentioned earlier, it does pay handsomely to include, where applicable, someone who is used to local politics and is knowledgeable about the workings of Local Authorities. The two Museums have both benefited from this to a considerable extent and with a little imagination, the idea can surely be used by quite different charities.

The Colonel-in-Chief of REME is HRH The Prince Philip, and it will be recalled that he is also the Captain General of The Royal Marines. He is fully cognizant of the neckties of regiments, and when I know he is going to officiate, it is often amusing to me (and I hope to him) to wear a Royal Marine tie at someone else's functions. When he officiated at the opening of REME's fine new Hall (The Prince Philip Hall) in Arborfield, he spent quite some time examining all the large 'antique' equipment and talking to all involved. When he came to talk to the Steering Committee members (and all such 'pow wows' are very light hearted) he saw my tie, and said, 'What the hell's a Marine doing here?' I briefly mentioned the Imperial War Museum and the Royal Marine Museum, and he said, 'Don't you ever go home?' 'Not often, Sir,' followed by a laugh – and that is as it should be. The publicity resulting from Royal attendance is of huge benefit to charities, and long may the Royal Family have the commitment and strength to keep the system in existence, demanding though it must be on all of them.

At the time of writing this (November 2000), a further surprise came in the post – a letter from the REME Corps Secretary (also a fellow Turner) asking if I would agree to accept honorary membership of the Royal Electrical & Mechanical Engineers Institution. This really did astonish me, and it was a privilege readily accepted. I have noticed that the 'outside' members of our Committee have all been so honoured, and that makes only twenty of us so appointed in eleven years. Another tie to be worn, with real pleasure, and again, long may these niceties be offered around. They are much appreciated and generally come right out of the blue!

Chapter Twenty-Three

The RAF Pathfinder Museum, 1999

Although the Pathfinder Museum is nothing to do with me, readers will now know of the fascination that grips me with Service museums. What happened here is somewhat different, but I hope this aside will demonstrate the need that I feel all people should recognize of preserving artefacts and things of considerable interest. Sadly they all too often land up on the bonfire, as happened with my Father's Royal Flying Corps memorabilia of World War I.

One of my friends, 'Buddy' Cunningham, joined the RAF in 1942, and after training, was posted to a Lancaster Bomber Squadron as a rear-gunner. The casualty rate was appalling; five raids was the average life of air crew. He survived forty-four raids, and after each one of these, he marked up a large map on which he had noted all the places bombed and the purpose behind the raids. This was of course strictly illegal, and I can only guess that if he had been found out he would have ended up behind the proverbial bars. When visiting the Pathfinder Museum at RAF Wyton, his wife pointed out the map which he had given to the Museum and said, 'What a pity he did not have it photographed to keep as a souvenir.' When speaking to the station commander I mentioned this to him, and told him of my interest in Service museums. I then asked him if he could have it photographed, and said I would give a small donation to their funds.

He agreed and more than kept to his word, sending me a large print and a smaller one. The wording on the map in the former was not totally clear, but the smaller one was much clearer. I had the smaller one framed and Buddy and Barbara came round to us for an evening, and as a 76th birthday present I gave them to him – he was somewhat 'gob-smacked'. Friendship is priceless and it is with gratitude that his service to our country is recorded in his Museum.

Chapter Twenty-Four

The Abbeyfield (Cheam) Society, 2000 to date

Although the name 'Abbeyfield' was not unknown, its activities meant virtually nothing to me until a year or so ago, when one of my sports club members asked me if I would consider becoming the Chairman. The reason was that following the death of the man who started this particular Society in 1980, one Austin Walker, the Executive Committee (all volunteers of course) were seeking assistance. My answer at that stage was 'nothing doing', because I had too much on my plate, but I did make the proviso that he could ask again in a year's time, when I had retired from two of my other much larger charities. He did ask again, and after discussions with him and other Trustees, it was made clear that this was not a job for life but for say three or four years; by that time eighty would be the next stop! As the charity is only two miles from home, I agreed, and since then the learning curve has been steep. I have been aided by willing help and advice from several Trustees whom I, or Cynthia, have known for very many years – one 'young lady' known by me sixty years ago, is still just as attractive as she was then, and the amount of work that they all do voluntarily is enormous. For those who perhaps do not know what Abbeyfield homes are, a short explanation will help readers to appreciate the amount of work that goes on in the homes and what is done for and on behalf of the residents.

To start with, let me say that the residents do actually pay for their rooms and all that goes with them. Each room is self-contained and the occupiers do get their own breakfast in the small 'galley area' in every room. The furniture is their own, and they can enjoy lunch and dinner in the dining room; all services are provided, including lifts, heating and lighting etc, but if they wish to have their room cleaned, they pay for that themselves. It is only when they are unable to look after themselves that they will have to move into other establishments that can cope with the disabilities that will inevitably come to most of us. We used to reckon on taking in applicants at around the ages of sixty or sixty-five, but this has risen to eighty or eighty-five or more, such is the change in life expectancy, and this will be debated later in the chapter on inflation and investment, which deals with the falling value of the pound and its damaging effect on cash resources of both charities themselves and the people who benefit by living in such houses

Thus the volunteers really do work very hard, and if a housekeeper, who is salaried, goes sick or who has the day off, volunteers will fill the gap if paid stand-in help is unavailable. It is this question that is generally beginning to cause real concern in all charities – as the older generation of volunteers fall off their perches, where are the new volunteers to be found?

You will by now wonder where we all go from here. Being a realist, which I am, and certainly neither a pessimist nor an optimist, things evolve. In our case, almost immediately after taking office, one of our residents sadly died and in his will he left us a huge legacy – enormous by any standards, amounting to some £1,800,000. Our job as Trustees, and mine as Chairman, is to find suitable ways of spending this money, and I can only estimate that it will take the best part of a couple of years to solve this interesting and totally unexpected problem. One topic that will be on the agenda is that of amalgamating with a neighbouring Abbeyfield, which perhaps is short of money. In any case, many are now finding that the position of Treasurer, Secretary and so on, can only be filled by paying a fee to the holders of those positions, and for the first time since Cheam Abbeyfield was founded, we have found ourselves in just that position. The new Treasurer is thus a debit item in our income and expenditure account, but, thank heavens and our legator, we can afford it.

In the Royal College of Radiologists I said I would not mention Oscar Craig again but another coincidence arises here. On becoming Chairman, I quickly learned that our Honorary Doctor was Oscar's wife, Dr Nancy Craig, who has now retired from The Abbeyfield

(Cheam) Society. The years 2001 and the following few years will, without doubt, be most interesting in our debates over what we might or might not be able to do with the sudden receipt of this large legacy, and I have said that my time ends in December 2002. By then we should have a clearer idea of what will be the needs of our residents in Abbeyfield Homes and what is the strength or otherwise in the number of volunteers.

CHAPTER TWENTY-FIVE

Charities: Conclusions & Views About the Future, 2000 - ?

THIS SECTION IS NOT of personal experience, much of which has been fully spelled out already. Obviously there is more – in fact much more – that can be said, but the flavours of the varying interests, the complexity of the problems, the decision-making that, hopefully, is more right than wrong, and the interweaving of views and personalities of all those involved have maintained interest to the full. This section is, I hope, a round-up of some of the changes and benefits that are currently affecting us all, and with luck may suggest some thoughts about the way ahead which will face every charity.

The activity of charities is legion and many have been started because of tragedy as a result of war and so on. The tax benefits of charities, which have lasted for centuries, have now been changed considerably and that subject will be debated in the next chapter or two, because income is being squeezed and that loss can only be replaced by new forms of fund-raising. This in itself is becoming more difficult because of the decreasing numbers of volunteers.

Thankfully, as disclosed in the section on 'Charities Aid Foundation', charities are still being created at a considerable rate – now some 8,000 a year – so philanthropy is thriving. Only relatively few people know the problems facing charities and there are some big guns amongst that number who work very hard to overcome the difficulties. If only that number could be multiplied by 10,000 or so, maybe politicians would take more notice. The tax changes of the last three years or so are depleting investment revenues to charities and their pension funds by an estimated £400,000,000 per year and either that revenue has to be replaced by another source of funding, or their services will inevitably be cut back. This has been touched upon at various times, but the serious point about it all is this: 'What services are charities being inveigled into doing, which had previously been carried out by Government, Local Authorities and the like?' It is not the duty of charities to take on the liabilities of Government. Into this scenario has to be put the problem of the vanishing volunteers and their replacement by paid 'staff'. Currently, it seems to me, two things are being tackled to assuage these matters, one being tax switches by the Government itself which has had to put back some of the revenue it has stolen from charities, and the other is an endeavour to encourage the British public to be more generous. It was mentioned in The Charities Aid Foundation section – and I make no apologies for repeating it – that we give only about one tenth of our personal income to charitable enterprises, in contrast to the United States of America, where the comparative figure is so much larger. Long-standing tax benefits for giving to charity have obviously deeply instilled the spirit of giving in America and I have to say that any effort to close this gap in Great Britain will take a very long time – if ever – to achieve an equal degree of generosity! We read very little about the new dot.com millionaires giving to charity, but I do hope they do; it is infectious, and I would like to see some of these wealthy people hitting the headlines in the press for generous giving, as in the past we have seen from such families and companies as Rowntree, Pilkington, Getty, Baring, Esmé Fairbairn and many others. In time, the lowering of the amounts of money that can be given by deed of gift (thus reducing the donor's tax bill) will be beneficial, but the burning question is 'how long will it take?' The reducing tax reclaim on dividends ends in 2004, so this has to be replaced by greater giving in order to balance the books, and it is this target which I feel is unlikely to be reached.

So what is it that has absorbed so much of my time and kept me busy? Having earned a living in the City of London handling the financial affairs of wealthy people, often those who gave quite large sums of money to charities and were heavily involved in charity work themselves, it followed that as my retirement drew near, some of these individuals sensed that I might have time on my hands. They thought it would help me and them if my energies could be switched in their direction, and that has certainly taken place. The key factor behind this change of direction has been the years in which they had seen investment performance producing increasing cash flow, and they seemed to recognize that my philosophy was simple and successful and that they, as Trustees, could sleep well in the belief that financial disaster of whatever magnitude was not likely to occur.

The precursor to handling funds that are likely to exist for far longer than any of us is to understand what inflation does to financial reserves, and it is this, and the investment decisions that follow, that is so fascinating – to me anyhow – but it matters not whose money it is; for a person with £50,000 spare for investment or for a charity with £50 million, the problem is the same in that 10% loss or gain is the same for each. Ten percent is ten percent however you look at it.

The end product of examining all the numbers has then to be converted into investment decisions. It is this jigsaw that so few people readily discuss and investment advice cannot be given unless family relationships and prospects are fully debated with advisers. Furthermore, the advisers themselves must be sound enough and painstaking enough to be able accurately to assess what ought to be done.

The next chapters will, hopefully, cover all this and other relevant matters and will give readers some nasty questions to fire at those who try to convince them that they are offering sound advice.

PART IV

Your Money – How Not to Lose It!

Chapter One

Introduction

'There are three ways to lose money:

The first is by gambling on horses which is the quickest way of doing it.

The second is by spending it on women which is by far the most pleasurable way, and

The third is by listening to experts which is without doubt the most certain'

Pompadour

It will be clear from all that has been written so far that my views on investment of money, and management of money, generally, are fairly strong and it is because of this that the world of 'charity moneys' has had such a fascination. I can only think that this keen interest has led others to ask me to join so many charity committees in various roles, and I trust that I have not let them down or given false recommendations too often. No one gets everything correct all the time, but if one is on the plus side of 50% there should not be too many regrets. All such decisions in charities should be made by committees and the trick is to get knowledgeable people on them. It has been highly enjoyable and, unlike competitive business, there has been no back-biting that I have come across. I will not say that the end is in sight for me, but it is undoubtedly far nearer than it was. The sums of money, from little beginnings, have become enormous, and so has the task grown similarly for all charities.

I am very concerned that the rules are changing – in some ways in a damaging direction. I understand the reasons, but bureaucrats are making the rules and often have not, on their side of the table, people who have been at the sharp end of the various types of work: they seem unable to appreciate the cost to charities of the huge increase in 'paper work' that in many cases surely cannot even be read, so great is the pile. I have, to my surprise, actually been somewhat complimentary at times in this writing, about the Charity Commission, but I have strong reservations about their role and that of the accountancy professions when it comes to the resultant large increases in costs of preparing annual accounts and the complexity of them, which lead to wrong impressions and statements in the press. My views are fairly well known by the Commission and I have no reason to think they will change, but those who agree with me (and many do) need to stand their ground so that costs can be cut and charity monies be used for charity.

My beliefs about money management in the investment field have stood the test of over fifty years and I cannot see, over the long term, why those views should change. Growth in all economies is the life blood of countries (and politicians!) and given that that is not going to change, it confirms my views and the views of those who taught me in the beginning, that equities have to be the winners; progress is progress. It goes in one direction in spite of the hurdles that have to be crossed, and will still have to be crossed *ad infinitum.*

My principal 'gripe' with the new rules is a technical one and I ask to be forgiven for putting it into print, but it needs to be stated. The value of an investment portfolio, if one is not intending to sell any of it, is irrelevant. The income from it is the true worth and not a paper figure which will rise or fall every day. What has now happened is that the *value* has to be put in the 'cash movement section' and when the market booms, it looks as though the charities have made a huge profit. This, in my view, puts off donors who might be intending to give money. Conversely, when the market falls, it will look as though a large loss has accrued when in reality nothing has changed. In December 1999 the FTSE 100 Index closed at a record 6920, and in December 2000 it had fallen to 6222 – a decline of 10%. This is so misleading to the mass of the public, who cannot see the wood for the trees.

So, the final part of this book is an attempt to explain what these views are in the hope that they will not only be of interest but, more to the point, may actually be of value to all who care to read about them. Much I hope is common sense, but money frightens many people; they do not like to show ignorance when seeking help, but as will be seen, so often the 'advisers' are not all that they pretend to be and neither have they the time to cover all that should be discussed. When you want them again in a few years' time, they are highly likely not to be found due to their companies being amalgamated, changes in communication such as high-tech developments, so that they will not be available for face-to-face discussions, or else they will have simply changed their jobs for whatever reason.

Most books written on the subject of money seem to have been by those who have made their fortunes; a few books have been written by those who have lost all their wealth, but the intention of this part of the book is somewhat different.

During a lifetime – over fifty years in fact – of looking after Pension Fund, Charity and other people's investments, there has always been the problem of telling clients that if it was that easy to make money, we would all have done it and retired early as multi-millionaires! That sadly is not the way life is for the vast majority of people. The trick is to hang on in real terms to what it has been one's good fortune to have in the first place. Hence the title of this section.

Very few people indeed actually start with nothing and by work alone end their lives with vast wealth. Most people who manage to save will have perhaps moderate amounts of money which they wish to take care of in order to produce an increasing flow of income after retirement.

One of the problems today, putting it bluntly, is that it is difficult to find any source of advice, and particularly on-going advice, for those who have say £50,000 to £100,000 to invest. The sum of money for any potential investor seeking advice has to be, to all intents and purposes, spare cash and it will almost certainly need to be invested for just two reasons: the first will be to produce an immediate and growing income and the second may well be to provide a source of immediately available cash for any number of multifarious reasons, be they planned or otherwise, to cover the emergencies that seem to come upon all of us from time to time. This part is certainly not written for experts to use as a 'bible' to predict the future when talking to their clients. Rather it is for those who frequently feel that they are being bamboozled by experts, when in truth they are only asking for some simple advice; they are given an instant answer which seems just too 'pat' to be true.

Hundreds of thousands of people will have, in later life, what seem to them to be quite large sums of cash which they ought to 'invest', and these sums will probably have come to them from sources such as legacies from their parents or the proverbial rich uncle or aunt. They may well have come to them at the age of sixty or sixty-five, when the day for retirement arrives and the commutation of part of the pension can be taken in a cash lump sum or, for the relatively few, it may simply have been won in a lottery or football pool or have come to them as a result of selling a business. In all these cases it will be quite likely that it is the first time in their lives that such sums of money will suddenly have become available.

When quite young, I can remember having a conversation with my father on the subject of money in the course of which I said that you needed money when you were young rather than when you were old. He was at the time doing some amateur plumbing and his reply has always stayed firmly in my mind. He said 'You need money when you are old, not when you are young – you need it to do what I am doing now and what I will not be able to do for myself much longer!' What was he doing? Standing on the 'loo' seat to fix a new washer to the old fashioned ball-cock, which in those days was eight feet or more above the floor! It is only now that the wisdom of that remark is hitting home quite hard, and as the population ages, so will more and more of us see this as a likely reality.

The following pages are therefore aimed at trying to put into simple language one or two truisms which many money managers may not choose to tell their clients, because the interests of both sets of people are poles apart. The client is really only interested in the long-term protection and growth of his or her money, and once an initial course of action has been agreed, the lack of subsequent activity will not in any way be able to earn the adviser the cash flow that is needed each year to make such a portfolio worth 'managing'.

The apt story to fit the situation is perhaps best described as the

INTRODUCTION

case of 'the tortoise and the hare'. So often, when it comes to investing money, the tortoise approach gives peace of mind and slow progress can, in fact, be very rewarding indeed over a passage of time, and will often beat switching investments and following 'fashion'.

As we can all expect nowadays to live longer than our ancestors, it is quite likely that following retirement we may have a life expectancy of twenty or thirty years. It could even be forty years – in other words, probably as long as we have lived in our working lives, and there is no point in living for retirement if retirement itself means that our hard-earned savings have been in the wrong place. Worse still will it be if they have been frittered away through bad advice or not enough attention being paid to the matter (possibly because of lack of interest). So it is vital that we should all try to look after such fortune as has come our way from whatever source.

One of the problems about 'money' and the proper planning in the use of it is that very little is taught in schools concerning the handling of money. Parents often seem loath to talk to their children about it (possibly because of the size of their overdrafts!). Thus it is perhaps not surprising that so few people have any real practical knowledge of what can be done – *and what should not be done* – with savings, which usually begin in small amounts. This latter point will be touched upon when debating the difference between unit trusts and investment trusts in the section, 'Free Advice'.

Another of the troubles is that over the last fifty years or so, we as a nation (and this goes for much of the rest of the world) have forgotten much about the old Scottish characteristic of 'thrift'. We have been carried away with the 'get rich quick' syndrome and this does not work.

What was for many years endemic high inflation may have had much to do with this attitude and we are currently seeing many examples of how disastrous this can be and so often is.

Inflation plays havoc with savings and for that reason alone I start by trying to translate that rather high-brow subject into everyday language which I hope will be readily understood. What follows is meant to be common sense and I hope that you find that it is so.

Since the end of the Second World War the value of the £1 has fallen dramatically. For those with long memories it can be recalled that many goods or services now cost some eighty to one hundred times their prices in 1950. That, in fact, does mean that the £1 of fifty years ago is now worth around 1.5p in 2000 money.

There was a brief spell in 1975 when inflation in the United Kingdom touched 27%; if that had continued for any length of time the £1 would have halved in value in a little over two and a half years. This really does demonstrate in a quite alarming fashion just what can happen, and why governments (and people) world-wide are so very concerned to see the problem resolved, although any solution is likely to cause considerable pain during the time it takes to achieve it.

This is not the only problem. Apart from any fall in eventual capital values, perhaps of even greater anxiety to many will be the fact that the much needed income will itself depreciate in real terms by a like amount, if invested in the wrong places. The combination of these two reductions will obviously compound the difficulty. As so many people have a real and justifiable aversion to selling investments and spending the capital, the squeeze on income can be more painful than the reduction in capital value, if not intending to realize any of it. If the capital *is not going to be spent*, our heirs will benefit at our current expense. This problem will be tackled later, but it is at that stage that individual preferences and wishes come into play.

There is a simple way of trying to assess this bit of mathematics which everyone can do for themselves.

The number '72' is the key – divide any anticipated constant rate of inflation into 72 and that gives the answer to how long it takes to halve any capital sum of money. For example, 7% inflation into 72 = 10 years to halve the starting figure; 10% takes 7 years, 5% takes 14 years. If living for say 30 years following retirement at 60 years of age, and one looks at 5% inflation, the damage results in cash in the bank or in fixed interest stocks falling to a value of 50% in real terms by age 74. It will fall in value a further 25% to 75% by age 88 – not a happy state of affairs.

CHAPTER THREE

Advice: Who Do You Believe and Where Do You Go?

IF THE EROSION OF capital values and the relative worth of 'income flows' makes depressing reading, and it does, the next and perhaps more readily appreciated hurdle to overcome is 'from where and from whom can unbiased advice be obtained?'

This is a constant query which always disturbs people who have money to invest, and as it is perhaps the question that is most frequently put to me, I have to say that it disturbs me as well. In short, it has to be said that it is difficult in the extreme, if not impossible, to obtain totally unbiased advice. This is where everybody should sit down and try to think through their problems before seeing, or even thinking of seeing, any 'expert'.

Those who may be approached for advice are likely to have a vested interest in seeing that the time which they spend in proffering that advice is paid for. Payment may not, in fact, be by way of a fee. It may be by way of a commission and those who receive those commissions may not be totally explicit in spelling out to the client concerned just what are the amounts involved. They may not be able, by the very nature of their job specification, to give advice on the whole range of investments that is available in the market. What is worse, they will almost certainly not know of the whole range in any case. This is hardly surprising as there are some thousands of authorised investment firms in business and far more than that in the number of stocks in which money can be invested.

Since 'big bang' in October 1986, the regulatory authorities under the control of the Securities Investment Board (SIB), now Financial Services Authority (FSA), have been struggling to find rules and regulations that are meant to overcome this very real problem. Some may say, without very much success so far.

What these new regulatory authorities have undoubtedly done is two things. First, they have made life so expensive for all those who are licensed to give advice, that the advisers need to earn considerable sums to pay these costs. Second, the additional behind-the-scenes costs that have had to be incurred to pay for all the back-office staff and paperwork that has to be kept up-to-date has also to be covered. This has made it inevitable that fees and commissions have had to escalate to such an extent that it does not readily pay many firms to give advice to clients whose savings are small in value. From the clients' point of view, how can it actually be proved, in money terms, that the advice was worth paying for anyway?

Yet again, as happens so often, it will pay all those with genuinely spare cash assets to sit down and try to use common sense. Much of what follows will be an attempt to point out the ways in which one's mind can be cleared in a logical way so that one will not be led down a path one did not intend to follow in the first place. Above all, do not lock up your money in such a way that you cannot get it back within a few weeks. This point – and I make no apologies for it – is very, very important. Just imagine locking up money in a five-year bond and then suddenly needing that cash to move house, for job purposes, and being unable to get at your cash. This did happen to one of my oldest friends after I told him not to do it.

The amalgamations of banks with insurance companies, stockbrokers with banks, insurance companies with insurance brokers etc. etc. mean that the salesmen and saleswomen are now more likely to be limited to selling products of their own companies or groups rather than giving general advice or 'best advice'. No longer are many consultants 'playing the field' and seeking, for a fee or commission, the best home for their clients' monies.

In short, the old fashioned friendly stockbroker or insurance broker who had time to chat over the telephone and who knew his clients personally has virtually disappeared, as I have mentioned before. Where then can the unfortunate customer go for advice?

Taking the easiest case first, it is those with the most cash for investment who will be most avidly sought after by any adviser. Those people will have the whole field in which to play. So what, one might ask, is the range of advisers? It is considerable, and everybody will seek to find the proverbial square peg for a square hole and not a round one. More often than not one should begin the fact-finding by writing, in the first instance, to the appropriate associations which cover the various groups of firms. The biggest and most powerful, and almost certainly the most expensive, will be the merchant banks, so a few words on each of several types of advisers should help.

Merchant Banks
The major City of London merchant banks, of which around a dozen were independent some ten years ago, have now nearly all been taken over by American and Continental banks or brokers. In either form they have been advising private clients for some sixty years or more, but particularly so since the end of the Second World War. Portfolio management grew out of the task that a few members of staff had been given (including me!), advising paternalistic directors on the day-to-day investment problems which arose on their own portfolios. These directors were too busy or otherwise occupied (hunting, shooting or fishing!) to take care of their portfolios themselves. Today the situation has changed dramatically, and the cost of running those prestigious and very expensive departments means that some merchant banks will only take on clients who have upwards of £1 million to invest. Others will look after sums of not less than £250,000 per client.

These customers will perhaps see their investment manager twice a year and a flat fee is likely to be charged of say £1 per £1,000 of value at each year-end valuation, with a minimum charge of perhaps £5,000 per year.

The results of such negotiations often depend very much on 'who or what you are.' These few words are given to begin a general but brief review of advisers by groups. Nevertheless, many people ask about merchant banks, and if interested enough, there is no harm in writing to them.

Investment Management Houses
This type of portfolio manager may well be running investment

trusts and/or unit trust management departments. They are also well known. Dependent upon the sums of money that one has, it is quite likely that you may, in the first instance, be steered towards their in-house trust vehicles for some or all of your money and then an independent portfolio could be added over the years as the sums of money available for investment increase.

Boutiques
This is a fairly recent description of companies quite often set up and run by executives who have, for their own satisfaction, decided to leave the very large houses and build their own more personalized businesses. This is very much the way these larger firms were in the early days of the 1950s, when friends who were stockbrokers acted on behalf of friends who did not know where to go for advice.

These advisers will also need to charge fees, but the starting figures can be much lower and certainly the amounts of money per client can fall to the £50,000 to £100,000 mark. For people who do not want to get involved in day-to-day management, or maybe are not even interested in financial matters, this type of manager is worth putting on the shopping list.

Stockbrokers
The financial world is nowadays such a rapidly changing place that the image of the old fashioned 'friendly' stockbroker has sadly become largely a thing of the past. Gone are the days when he (and it really would then have been 'he') would have had time to spend a quarter of an hour on the telephone talking about nothing very much and then having, perhaps, a single order for a £5,000 transaction, Today, a broker is as cost-conscious as anyone else in the City of London and that person's time represents money. It can also prove costly to the client because small orders are relatively expensive.

Joint Stock Banks (Clearing Banks)
Before 'big bang' in October 1986, the local bank manager would almost certainly have known most of his customers quite well, and anybody could see him or telephone him just to talk about the money

that was available for investment or might become available. The manager, having ascertained to what use the money was going to be put, would then have telephoned that branch's stockbroker in order to place the buying or selling orders. The size of the transaction was irrelevant.

Today the re-organizing of the structure of the clearing banks has led to considerable dismay as perceived by many customers, who now find themselves cut off from the old-fashioned personal touch. In order to get any advice at all they may have to telephone people they have never spoken to before, and they will be all too well aware that the bank official at the other end of the telephone does not know them either and certainly will have no personal background knowledge of the customer's likes and dislikes – or indeed his needs or prospects.

In the race for business, the clearing banks have set up, at great expense, their own securities and dealing departments, in effect taking the place of the stockbrokers of old; the costs of dealing have of course risen, partly to cover their own expenses.

What is playing safe?
For those who have less than perhaps £50,000 free capital with which to invest in stocks and shares or gilt edged securities or building societies, it has to be understood that it is quite justifiable to have a portfolio consisting solely of shares for such an amount of money, as has been the case with many people taking up shares in de-nationalized companies. The holdings would not number as many as there would be in a more wealthy person's portfolio and the costs of dealing in small amounts are relatively expensive. This means that the spread of risk may not be very great, and, whilst concentrating portfolios into few stocks can be beneficial at times, there are other occasions when the swings and roundabouts work to one's disadvantage. For such amounts of money it is well worth considering the advantages of investing in investments trusts or unit trusts. The differences between these two types of investment vehicles are important and are explained later.

It can thus be seen how difficult it is for 'beginners' to enter the very interesting world of investment in stocks and shares. The word 'beginners' can be used to describe both people who suddenly have large sums of money at their disposal, as well as those who save money slowly, beginning possibly by placing money on deposit in banks and building societies and then gradually becoming bolder and wishing to invest in stock markets at a later date.

What has not been touched upon is the way in which bank deposit accounts and building society deposits compare with British Government (Gild-Edged) issues. The differences between the relative performance of various classes of investments will be examined in the light of inflation and the movements of stock markets. In fact it will be revealed that the advantages of equities over other forms of investment have greatly outweighed the disadvantages. Each investor will have to make up his or her own mind as to which avenue he or she would choose to follow. Of prime importance for each person is that he or she must have confidence in his or her choice of the way forward. They must be able to sleep well on their decisions. There is absolutely no point in having money and then worrying about it.

Before actually deciding how much you might wish to commit to the market of your choice, you must be quite clear about what is going to happen to your money. Apart from the choice of direction in which you wish your cash to be invested, the next most important point to realize is that, even in good times, stock markets of all sorts can go down as well as up. Therefore, investors should never look for short-term rewards. They may of course happen to be some of the lucky few who, quite by accident, will have bought shares just before a take-over announcement or some other news of great importance, but that would be a most unexpected bonus. In spite of what you may read, this type of occurrence is very rare indeed.

Free Advice
If some of the following points have been covered before, I make no apology for mentioning any of them again, because they are very important. There is a way of obtaining 'free' advice about investing money in the stock market, and that is by writing to, or telephoning,

one or two of the major unit trusts or investment trusts. Ask them to send you a copy of their annual report and accounts and, usually near the end, there is a schedule of the investments held by them. Admittedly, what is seen may be six months old, but the largest twenty or so holdings will be 'core stocks' and if only because of their very size, are almost certainly long-term holdings.

Some of these unit trusts will have a method of subscribing regularly for new shares, and these subscriptions can be as little as £50 a month. Over a period of years such an amount (£600 pa) will be regularly invested whatever the level of the market, and this system is what is known as 'averaging'. This gets round the problem of intending investors having to guess whether the market is high, low, going up or going down. When wishing to 'go it alone' and invest some money oneself after a few years, the readers of those reports will have seen what the professionals are doing, and one very good bit of advice given to me in the 1960s was 'follow the money'. For major companies this is fine, but for new fashions, such as high-tec companies, this is not for 'Widows and orphans'.

My own preference, which has been touched upon, is to keep to 'high cash flow' companies, rather than long-contract companies, such as engineering. My fixation has been limited to things that everybody does or uses, such as banks, insurance companies, financial advisers, stores shares, petroleum companies, pharmaceutical companies and a few specialist areas with seemingly exponential growth, such as BAA (British Airports Authority) and food shares. All of these will have periods of growth and setback, so try to follow the papers and see if purchases can be made at the bottom of a cycle rather than the top!

I mention, one last time, that the long-term holding is so often more rewarding than trying to guess short-term movements, and if one has really got a winner in a portfolio, I have never subscribed to the view of 'taking the top off it' – one is likely to reinvest in a second eleven stock and switching is expensive. Even experts get this wrong from time to time as, we all know!

Investment Trusts versus Unit Trusts

This seems a suitable place in which I can expand upon references made about these two types of investment vehicles.

Unit Trusts

This is the more simple avenue to explore first, and it is particularly so when investors are thinking of investing, say £50 or £100 a month, perhaps for many years ahead. Most trusts will accept such payments, and one only has to look at the weekend broadsheet newspapers to see frequent references to them and the addresses and telephone numbers will be there for all to see. The system operated is simple, in that the total portfolio value (from perhaps 100 different shares in their portfolio) is divisible by the number of units sold and held by investors. This value is calculated daily, weekly, or whenever specified by the Trust itself, and when new units are purchased by investors, it is at that price at which new units are valued, subject to a spread in price, which is slightly higher if purchasing units, and slightly lower if selling units.

For larger sums of money, on a one-off basis, exactly the same system applies. Dividends can be paid direct to one's bank account, or some trusts will permit those dividends to be used to purchase further new shares. These trusts are technically known as 'open ended', in that expansion through sales of new units is unlimited.

Investment Trusts

The principle is similar in only one respect: shares in such companies are backed by that Company's own investment portfolio of, say, the same 100 companies' shares as in the Unit trusts. That is the only bit that is similar, and which is in effect the same for an investor, covered as they are by a broad list of different shares.

The difference is that these trusts are 'closed ended.' That is, they do not issue or redeem their own shares when investors try to purchase or sell shares. They are limited companies, and one has to buy (or sell) existing shares from current shareholders. Thus, there is a 'demand' factor in the equation, and frequently Investment Trust shares are priced at a discount to the full value of the underlying assets (net asset value – NAV). This is likely to earn investors a slightly higher return in income than unit trusts, but the converse is that it is not so easy to buy and sell shares, and small purchases and sales can be more expensive in costs and freedom to deal.

Investors should always look a long way down the track and, as a minimum it would be wise to consider looking not less than, say, five years ahead, for real evidence of growth in both capital and income returns. Therefore, full allowance must be made, by retaining sufficient cash on deposit in a bank or building society, for such things as a new car, a daughter's or son's wedding, moving house or extending your existing home (not forgetting all the on-costs involved by way of new furnishings and so on). It also has to be said that allowance should be made for personal problems such as sudden disasters to one's family or property – in other words unforeseen liabilities should always be covered by having sufficient cash readily available.

For those who have already been investors, however small and for however many years, they will well understand the temptation to say to themselves: 'My new lounge suite will cost £2,500 and if I wait before selling my shares, their value may well rise £500 and that will be of great help.' Do not ever think like that. If only that could happen every time, we would all have made our fortunes, but life is not like that; it is a fair bet that between ordering your new furniture and having to sell in order to pay the bill, the share prices will have fallen and the mental agony and loss of sleep through worrying about this increasing shortfall in cash is simply not worth it. This can be called 'sod's law' because that is what it is and it happens so often!

The answer to this predicament is easy: sell your shares, count up the cash which results, place your order for the furniture and in the meantime benefit from the interest which will accrue from the deposit account until the furniture arrives.

It is only after all possible contingencies have been thought through that cash should be committed to the stock markets, so where to begin?

So often clients and potential clients (and friends) say, 'I must play safe with my money and I would like to put it all in a building society or in Government Stocks (Gilt-Edged securities), where I know it is safe and I can rely on guaranteed income.'

The first point about that statement is that it is not correct. Certainly one can rely on a fixed rate of interest return from British Government securities for a time and an investor can calculate an annual and constant return on his or her money based on the yield at the time of purchase. This will only last for as long as the stock itself exists.

Apart from the very few undated gild-edged stocks, all current and post-war Government securities have dates attached to them when they will be repaid. It will help to explain that all such stocks are repaid at £100% on a given date in the future (may be as far as twenty years away) and care must be taken on two points. The first is that if the stock is bought at £115 per £100 of stock the repayment date will produce for the investor a cash repayment of only £100. Thus for every £100 of stock purchased there will be a loss of £15, but perhaps of greater importance will be the fact that when you come to reinvest the proceeds, you may find that money rates will have fallen and that you cannot replace the income you will have lost. Thus an investor can only rely on a fixed return for a given period of years and then a re-assessment has to take place – and that could be painful indeed.

In the case of a building society deposit (other than for a year or two) the rates will always go up and down with the movements in money rates generally, and these movements can be quite severe. No fixed estimate for income from any building society, or bank for that matter, can be calculated with any degree of accuracy for longer than a very short time. Long-term holders of building society or bank deposits should certainly consider investing such sums into the stock market.

When it comes to buying British ordinary shares, the picture is quite different, because in recent years it has become customary for any selection of shares to return a yield less than that obtainable from Gilt-Edged stocks or building society deposits at the time the investment is made. The attraction of shares is that in time there will be growth in the dividends – and that growth in itself always raises the capital values of shares as is clearly visible from Tables I and II.

Table I: Real Investment Returns (% pa)

Last	2000	10 yrs	20 yrs	50 yrs	101 yrs
Equities	–8.6	11.8	11.8	7.7	5.5
Gilts	6.1	9.4	7.7	1.2	1.1
Corporate Bonds	4.8	10.5			
Index-Linked	0.1	6.2			
Cash	3.2	4.2	4.7	1.4	0.9

Table II: Real Investment Returns (% pa)

	Equities	Gilts	Index-Linked	Cash
1901-10	4.0	–0.1		1.9
1911-20	–7.9	–10.8		–6.3
1921-30	12.8	13.1		9.8
1931-40	2.3	4.0		–1.2
1941-50	6.3	0.3		–1.1
1951-60	12.1	–4.1		–0.6
1961-70	3.3	–1.4		1.6
1971-80	0.4	–3.2		–3.1
1981-90	11.7	6.0		5.2
1991-00	11.8	9.4	6.2	4.2

Source: Barclays Capital

Since the Second World War, the United Kingdom has lived through many and varied crises, including for example three separate spells of Conservative and Labour administrations, Suez, fuel crises, several devaluations, the intervention of the International Monetary Fund (IMF), strikes of varying lengths and severity, the Falklands War and the Middle East conflicts and many other items of good and bad news.

Given all these factors, we might be forgiven for thinking that the financial markets had all been gloom and doom, but that is most definitely not so. It now seems appropriate to examine what has actually happened to Gilt-Edged stocks and British equities markets over varying spells of time covering over fifty years. This is best shown in graph form because a spell of years can be seen at one glance, rather than having to plough through masses of figures.

Table III: Barclays Total Return Indices: Nominal Terms, Gross Income Reinvested

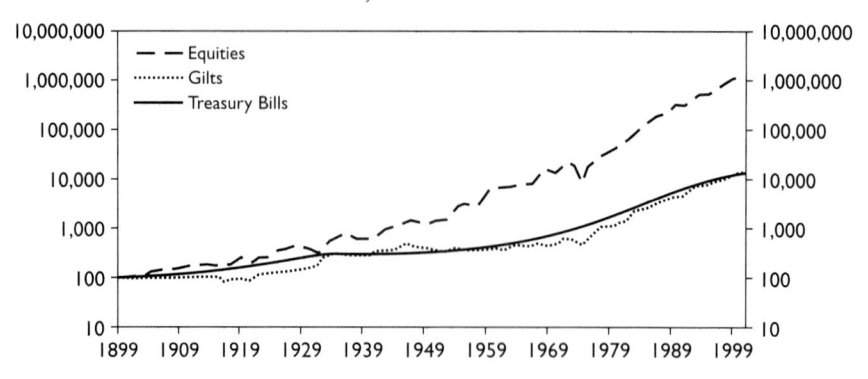

Barclays Price Indices: £100 Nominal Since 1945

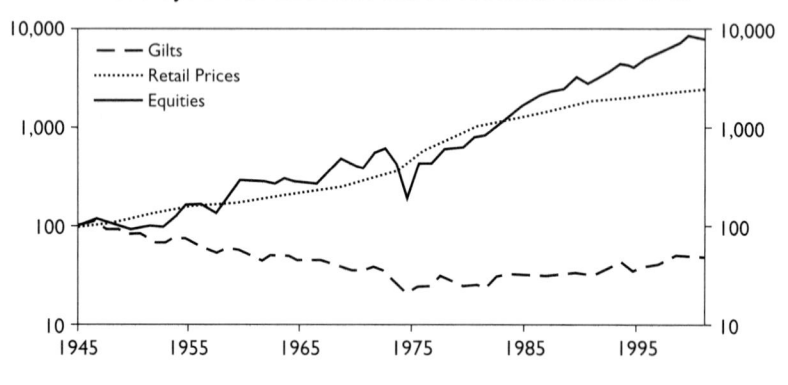

Source: Barclays Capital

Chapter Four

The Performance of Government Stocks and Equities

So OFTEN THERE IS one major criticism that can be made about any exercise of trying to prove a point over the relative performance of investing in one particular market or adviser versus another and it is worth giving some time to this matter. The complaint that can be levied is that a writer of any article, or the giver of any lecture, is picking certain times to suit his or her particular argument. Criticism can sometimes be fully justified, particularly when listening to politicians!

When it comes to our own money, these points suddenly become very meaningful and the doubts become particularly relevant. In order to overcome this criticism, there are set out in this section various tables which begin well before the famous 'crash of October 1974' and the smaller setback of 1987, when the market was at or near one of its all-time peaks up to that date. It is worth repeating the table from page 199:

Table IV: Real Investment Returns (% pa)

	Equities	Gilts	Index-Linked	Cash
1901-10	4.0	–0.1		1.9
1911-20	–7.9	–10.8		–6.3
1921-30	12.8	13.1		9.8
1931-40	2.3	4.0		–1.2
1941-50	6.3	0.3		–1.1
1951-60	12.1	–4.1		–0.6
1961-70	3.3	–1.4		1.6
1971-80	0.4	–3.2		–3.1
1981-90	11.7	6.0		5.2
1991-00	11.8	9.4	6.2	4.2

Source: Barclays Capital

Table V: Equity Risk Premium Excess: Returns of Equities Relative to Gilts (5 years annualized)

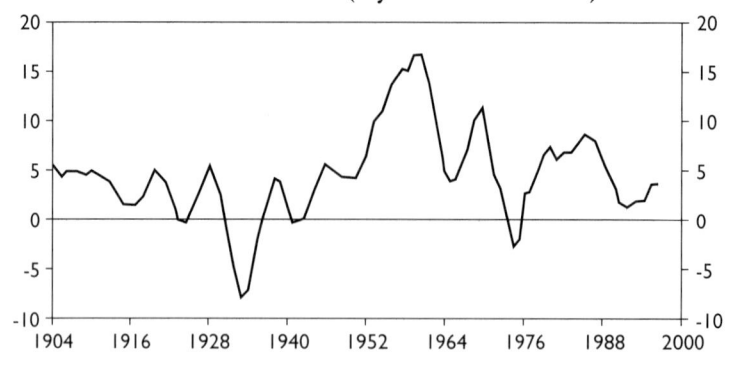

Table VI: Barclays Price Indices: Nominal Terms

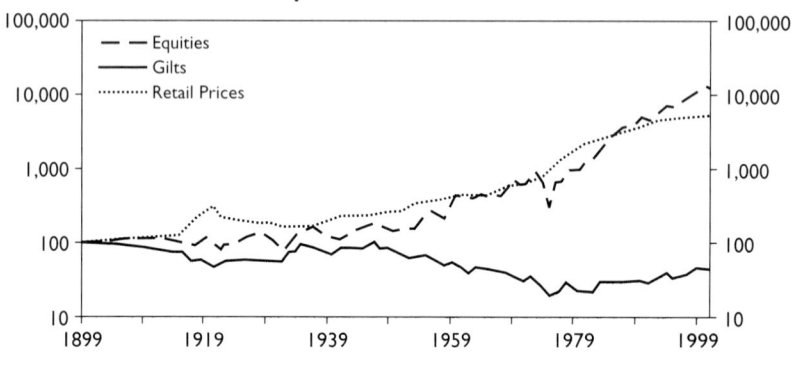

Table VII: Barclays Total Return Indices: Nominal Terms Since 1945

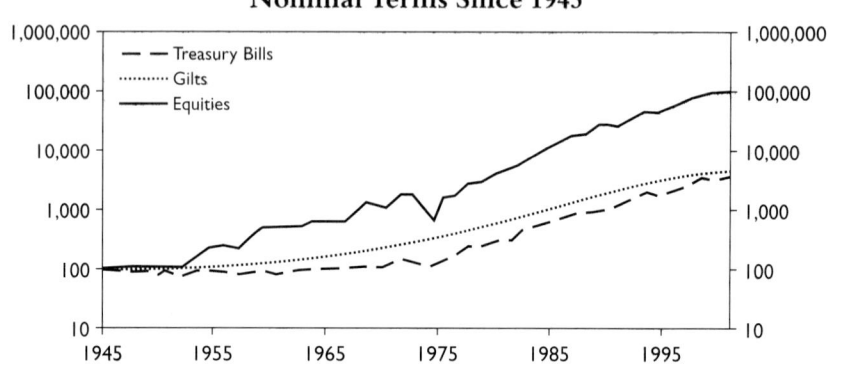

Source: Barclays Capital

Table VIII: Value of £100 Invested at the End of 1945

Income Reinvested Gross

	Nominal	Real
Equities	£ 97,023	£ 4,132
Gilts	£ 3,296	£ 140
Cash	£ 4,165	£ 177

Without Reinvesting Income

	Nominal	Real
Equities	£ 7,727	£ 329
Gilts	£ 49	£ 2

Table IX: Value of £100 Invested at the End of 1899

Income Reinvested Gross

	Nominal	Real
Equities	£ 1,209,836	£ 22,817
Gilts	£ 15,350	£ 289
Cash	£ 13,601	£ 257

Without Reinvesting Income

	Nominal	Real
Equities	£ 12,329	£ 233
Gilts	£ 45	£ 1

Table X: Value of £100 Invested at the End of 1990

Income Reinvested Gross

	Nominal	Real
Equities	£ 405	£ 306
Gilts	£ 324	£ 245
Index-Linked Gilts	£ 242	£ 182
Treasury Bills	£ 200	£ 151
Corporate Bonds	£ 361	£ 272

Source: Barclays Capital

Dividends have fallen as a proportion of total returns for equities, and 2000 marked a new low for their contribution. The abolition of the ACT tax credit and the higher proportion of newer, non- or low-dividend paying companies in the equity index have both played their part in recent years. The UK is also buying into the 'cult of the buy-back', following the US trend of returning cash to shareholders via share buy-backs, rather than through less fashionable, and less tax-efficient, dividends. *Equity investors are now more dependent than ever upon capital appreciation.*

The above graphs and figures have all been extracted from the Annual Equity-Gilt Study 2001, which, in its earlier days, was produced by the stockbrokers de Zoete & Bevan, then in its later name of Barclays de Zoete Wedd (BZW) and later still with its new name. It is now published by Barclays Capital. My final extract from their publication is in the appendix section at the back of this book in Appendix A. This is really for the statisticians, but the figures are well worth a brief study because each year of the category is there for everyone to see, and they may help to comfort readers that doomsday has not yet arrived. On top of my earlier comments about the ups and downs of the United Kingdom economy, we have survived two world wars, and they surely have put the doomsters in their place. Investment in equities, over the long view, is not a risk, if a broad portfolio is held, but let the figures speak for themselves.

My last comments about managing one's own financial affairs refer to family wealth, or lack of it.

Chapter Five

Personal Financial Planning

Although things are slowly improving, it has always appalled me that families do not communicate about money and I blame the education system for this. My wife Cynthia did Citizens Advice Bureau work for twenty-five years, and occasionally I was told horrendous stories (no names of course) about debt problems where perhaps eight or more credit cards were sizeably in the red. How can people do such a thing when surely all must know that the debts have to be paid off – or else? At the other end of life it has always left me speechless when talking to clients that they have not written their wills, and seem so often to have their houses registered incorrectly. Many will say that their homes are taken care of because they have registered their property in joint names. Nonsense I say. The house should be registered as 'tenants in common', where both partners are named. By this means, when the death of one occurs, that half of the house can be willed separately and does not go into the survivor's possession. It does not affect the inhabiting of the house but it does mean that half of its value (say £200,000 out of £400,000) is thus already taken care of when the survivor dies. In simple language, it will save death duty up to the duty free allowance as decreed in the Budget of the day which is currently some £250,000. That means, at 40% duty, a net £100,000 saving to the family. In the last six months I have had to post to three friends, all senior men in business, the rules which they had never heard about.

This, in my view, is a failing of major severity when one pays for advice, and frankly it is often not given. I told my friends to go back and get the next bit of advice free!

It is the summation of all these views, gained by long experience of handling monies of all sizes for all types of clients, that has solidified my thoughts on how money should be invested, and it is this perhaps above anything else that has involved me in so many differing types of problems with charities. Trustees should have someone with them who understands finance and who can therefore keep things on the straight and narrow. It is partly for this reason that I have tried to spell out in this part some basic principles which ought to help. One Trustee in a charity which had received a seven-figure legacy out of the blue asked, 'Could we have a new bird bath?' This, I think, is a good example of what I have been trying to spell out in the last few pages.

Part V

Sport and Family Life

CHAPTER ONE

Sport – Cheam Fields Club

APART FROM SPORTING ACTIVITIES mentioned in earlier chapters, I thought a few words should be added about how I learned a few lessons in 'man (or woman!) management' at the sharp end.

As was mentioned in the first chapter, we lived opposite a small sports club (Cheam Fields) from 1928 to 1962. I joined as a junior tennis member in 1935, aged ten, and am now the longest-ever continuous full-playing member. Fifty years ago, because I suppose of my natural inquisitiveness at the beginning, I became a member of the General Committee, beginning on return from the War in 1946 until I bowed out a year or so ago at age seventy-five.

During that time, in various spells of office, I was:-
President in three spells	for fifteen years
Chairman in two spells	for fourteen years
Honorary Treasurer	for five years
Tennis Secretary	for four years
Social Secretary in three spells	for five years

and over those years we converted our three grass courts into hard courts (sacrilege!), extended the Club House and living quarters three times, and in real terms have spent something like £250,000 and now have virtually no debt.

It is obvious, from this brief outline, just how many meetings we all attended, and how great were the decisions to be made. We are a very unusual club because it just exists! There are no shareholders, so we are a 'members club' which is now nearly ninety years old; some members have been generous in the extreme and very rarely have we ever had difficulty with members. The sport is confined to tennis and bowls in the summer, and in winter indoor activities include short mat bowls, bridge, darts, table tennis etc – all is serious fun and even

Cheam Fields Club. The Three Champions, 1950.

the competitions are (usually) truly sporting ones. Most of us, of course, lose most of the time, but we do our best, and both major sports from time to time have produced county wins and colours for the few.

All this is 100% voluntary, and it will be a sad day if we ever have to pay committee members. Rather like charities (for this is almost what we are), volunteers are vital, and so far we have been able to find them – long may that continue.

Out of so many funny incidents, just one story. A president in the 1960s was a local solicitor who had the best collection of stories (not clean ones!) of anyone I have ever met. He was of short build and after a furious argument at a General Committee Meeting, he said angrily to me, 'For two pins I would stand up and take you on.' Then, a moment later, he added, 'Perhaps you think I am standing up!' Laughter ensued – he was a great friend, a successful sportsman and sadly, yet another loss because he died a couple of years ago having reached ninety not out.

All this committee work is a real way to learn how far you can go in committee and, to put one on the learning curve, there surely is no better way than being at the sharp end of sports clubs committee work. I recommend it to anyone!

As a final 'stop-press', a pleasant surprise came along in the spring of 2001. The Surrey County Bowling Association give an award for those who have done long spells of work for their clubs. Some six or so of these awards are given each year. In May the President came to us and presented me with a badge for the Bowls Blazer plus a certificate. Rather as in the picture on the previous page, we had another round of beer!

Chapter Two

The Family

It takes two to tango, and in Cynthia I have had the perfect partner. In 2002, if both still on this earth, we shall celebrate fifty years of very happy married life. Of course there are always problems and they have to be debated and overcome, but we have been lucky with our health (a lottery) and fortunately our children, Nicola in Australia with her family, and John, only a few miles away with his wife Christina, are equally fit and long may that continue. During these years, we had, as I said at the beginning, perfect relationships with our respective 'in-laws' and have always lived within a few hundred yards of each other. I know everyone says that you pick your friends but not your relatives. In our case we had both in one, and advice and help was always literally next door. Once the children left home, Cynthia steered her own course by changing direction into voluntary work, beginning almost at the same time in the Sutton Citizens Advice Bureau where she stayed twenty-five years, as has already been mentioned. Her Arthritis Research Campaign work as Secretary or Chairman has now lasted over thirty years. In both cases her experience has to some extent paralleled my own. We have both have been frustrated by officialdom, notably in filling in forms when one should be helping people, a practice which has been taken too far. Maybe it is our age catching up with us, but I do not think so. Endless time spent waiting on the telephone, pressing buttons when trying to speak to someone, only to find that they are out and 'please try again' – maybe the younger generation just accept it as a way of life.

It might appear that our lives have been all work and no play, but that is totally wrong. Firstly, because we have been able to spend much time in the USA and Canada for work and without having to pay the air fares (we have to now) and secondly we were able to

Ballarat, Australia. With the last working goldminer.

Arches National Park, Utah, USA.

Alaska. Before canoeing to glacier face.

Alaska. On a glacier and about to dog-sledge, 1990s. Cynthia seated.

continue those trips by taking holidays afterwards. Thus we did for a spell spend a month a year 'over the pond', mostly aiming for the Rockies. Altogether we have driven cars over 51,000 miles in those countries. In Australia we have also spent some few weeks, at least once every eighteen months since 1982, visiting the family in Sydney, with breaks in New Zealand. We have flown in Concorde (without bits dropping off!); have been some one hundred feet down in a submarine looking at wrecks, fish and coral; and panned for gold and found $50 worth between us in Alaska. I have been to the coal face in Wales, used a drill for gold in South Africa, been to the Falklands, and we spent ten days in the Kakadu at the 'top end' of Australia. That indeed is a very different place to go and there is one thing certain about that area: crocodiles abound and one does not wander off on one's own – especially at night!

Our aim has been to get out into the sticks, and for some strange reason to do it ourselves. That way you do not have to get up too early in the morning to catch a coach to wherever with dozens of other people. We have always 'found the natives' friendly and helpful. We have taken hundreds of photographs and many videos and very seldom look at any of them, but the memories are great and we would do it again.

The lottery of life has been kind to us, but would it have been better by turning left or right at times? I doubt it. It has been fun, and the game, we trust, is not yet finished – love all will be a good score! I for one would do it all again, and that I think sums it up – so far!

Appendix A

UK Cost of Living Index and Other Indices

UK Cost of Living Index

Year	Dec (1899=100)	Change % In Year	Change % Five-Year Average	Year	Dec	Change % In Year	Change % Five-Year Average
1900	103	3.3					
1901	103	0.0		1951	294	12.0	5.3
1902	107	3.2		1952	313	6.3	6.0
1903	107	0.0		1953	316	1.1	5.2
1904	107	0.0	1.3	1954	329	4.0	5.3
1905	107	0.0	0.6	1955	348	5.8	5.8
1906	100	−6.2	−0.7	1956	358	3.0	4.0
1907	110	10.0	0.6	1957	375	4.6	3.7
1908	113	3.0	1.2	1958	382	1.8	3.9
1909	113	0.0	1.2	1959	382	0.0	3.1
1910	113	0.0	1.2	1960	389	1.8	2.3
1911	117	2.9	3.1	1961	406	4.4	2.5
1912	120	2.9	1.8	1962	416	2.6	2.1
1913	120	0.0	1.1	1963	424	1.9	2.1
1914	120	0.0	1.1	1964	445	4.8	3.1
1915	148	23.6	5.5	1965	465	4.5	3.6
1916	176	18.5	8.6	1966	482	3.7	3.5
1917	213	20.9	12.1	1967	493	2.5	3.4
1918	245	15.2	15.3	1968	523	5.9	4.3
1919	250	2.3	15.8	1969	547	4.7	4.2
1920	299	19.6	15.1	1970	590	7.9	4.9
1921	221	−26.0	4.7	1971	644	9.0	6.0
1922	200	−9.5	4.2	1972	693	7.7	7.0
1923	197	4.7	−4.3	1973	766	10.6	7.9
1924	201	2.3	−4.3	1974	913	19.1	10.8
1925	197	−2.2	−8.0	1975	1140	24.9	14.1
1926	199	1.1	−2.1	1976	1312	15.1	15.3
1927	188	−5.6	−1.3	1977	1471	12.1	16.3
1928	187	−0.6	−1.0	1978	1594	8.4	15.8
1929	186	−0.6	−1.6	1979	1869	17.2	15.4
1930	172	−7.2	−2.6	1980	2152	15.1	13.5
1931	165	−4.5	−3.7	1981	2411	12.0	12.9
1932	159	−3.4	−3.3	1982	2542	5.4	11.6
1933	159	0.0	−3.2	1983	2677	5.3	10.9
1934	160	0.7	−2.9	1984	2799	4.6	8.4
1935	164	2.1	−1.1	1985	2959	5.7	6.6
1936	168	2.7	0.4	1986	3069	3.7	4.9
1937	178	6.0	2.3	1987	3182	3.7	4.6
1938	174	−2.5	1.8	1988	3398	6.8	4.9
1939	192	10.9	3.7	1989	3659	7.7	5.5
1940	217	12.7	5.8	1990	4001	9.3	6.2
1941	224	3.1	5.9	1991	4180	4.5	6.4
1942	222	−0.5	4.6	1992	4288	2.6	6.1
1943	221	−0.5	5.0	1993	4369	1.9	5.2
1944	224	1.0	3.0	1994	4496	2.9	4.2
1945	226	1.0	0.8	1995	4640	3.2	3.0
1946	227	0.5	0.3	1996	4754	2.5	2.6
1947	234	3.2	1.0	1997	4927	3.6	2.8
1948	246	4.9	2.1	1998	5062	2.8	3.0
1949	254	3.5	2.6	1999	5151	1.8	2.8
1950	262	3.2	3.0	2000	5302	2.9	2.7

Barclays UK Equity Index

Year	Equity Price Index December		Equity Income Index December		Income Yield %	Equity Price Index Adjusted for Cost of Living		Equity Income Index Adjusted for Cost of Living	
1899	100		100			100		100	
1900	108	+8.3%			6.3	105	+4.8%		
1901	100	−7.9%	69	−30.6%	4.8	97	−7.9%	69	−30.6%
1902	101	+1.3%	80	+15.6%	5.4	95	−1.9%	78	+11.9%
1903	98	−2.7%	66	−17.3%	4.6	92	−2.7%	64	−17.3%
1904	106	+8.0%	62	−6.1%	4.0	100	+8.0%	60	−6.1%
1905	105	−0.7%	71	+13.7%	4.6	99	−0.7%	69	+13.7%
1906	112	+6.1%	77	+8.5%	4.7	112	+13.2%	79	+15.7%
1907	107	−4.7%	79	+2.9%	5.1	97	−13.3%	74	−6.4%
1908	108	+1.3%	57	−27.4%	3.6	95	−1.7%	52	−29.5%
1909	115	+6.3%	73	+26.5%	4.3	101	+6.3%	66	+26.5%
1910	112	−2.1%	69	−4.5%	4.2	99	−2.1%	63	−4.5%
1911	109	−2.9%	71	+2.1%	4.4	94	−5.7%	63	−0.8%
1912	108	−1.4%	69	−3.2%	4.4	90	−4.2%	59	−5.8%
1913	100	−7.1%	57	−16.5%	3.9	83	−7.1%	49	−16.5%
1914	96	−4.4%	57	+0.1%	4.1	80	−4.4%	49	+0.1%
1915	96	0.0%	36	−37.8%	2.6	64	−19.1%	25	−49.7%
1916	89	−6.8%	67	+88.2%	5.2	51	−21.4%	39	+58.8%
1917	93	+4.2%	66	−2.2%	4.8	44	−13.8%	32	−19.1%
1918	108	+16.3%	63	−3.6%	4.0	44	+1.0%	27	−16.3%
1919	116	+7.7%	34	−47.0%	2.0	46	+5.3%	14	−48.2%
1920	86	−25.6%	77	+128.9%	6.1	29	−37.8%	26	+91.4%

222

Year	Equity Price Index December		Equity Income Index December		Income Yield %	Equity Price Index Adjusted for Cost of Living		Equity Income Index Adjusted for Cost of Living	
1921	80	−7.1%	79	+2.7%	6.7	36	+25.5%	37	+38.8%
1922	96	+19.8%	73	−7.9%	5.2	48	+32.5%	37	+1.8%
1923	92	−4.0%	72	−0.8%	5.3	47	−2.4%	38	+0.9%
1924	106	+15.3%	67	−7.5%	4.3	53	+12.8%	34	−9.5%
1925	117	+9.9%	73	+10.3%	4.3	59	+12.4%	39	+12.7%
1926	119	+1.8%	83	+12.5%	4.8	60	+0.7%	43	+11.2%
1927	124	+4.0%	76	−8.2%	4.2	66	+10.1%	42	−2.8%
1928	139	+12.2%	79	+3.9%	3.9	74	+12.9%	44	+4.5%
1929	113	−19.1%	90	+14.9%	5.5	61	−18.6%	50	+15.6%
1930	102	−9.2%	80	−11.0%	5.4	59	−2.1%	48	−4.2%
1931	77	−24.3%	65	−18.7%	5.8	47	−20.8%	41	−14.8%
1932	99	+27.9%	64	−2.4%	4.4	62	+32.4%	41	+1.0%
1933	119	+20.6%	60	−5.6%	3.5	75	+20.6%	39	−5.6%
1934	131	+9.8%	70	+15.7%	3.6	82	+9.0%	45	+14.9%
1935	144	+9.9%	78	+11.5%	3.7	88	+7.7%	49	+9.2%
1936	166	+15.1%	82	+5.8%	3.4	99	+12.1%	51	+3.0%
1937	138	−16.7%	93	+12.7%	4.6	78	−21.4%	54	+6.4%
1938	118	−14.9%	94	+1.8%	5.5	68	−12.7%	56	+4.4%
1939	114	−3.1%	90	−4.8%	5.4	59	−12.6%	48	44.2%
1940	102	−10.2%	94	+4.8%	6.3	47	−20.3%	45	−7.1%
1941	119		91		5.2	53		42	
1942	135	+31.8%	86	−7.9%	4.4	61	+28.5%	40	−10.2%
1943	144	+7.1%	86	−0.2%	4.1	65	+7.7%	40	+0.3%
1944	156	+8.3%	87	+0.4%	3.8	70	+7.3%	40	−0.6%
1945	160	+2.0%	88	+2.0%	3.8	71	+1.0%	40	+1.0%
1946	182	+13.9%	93	+4.9%	3.5	80	+13.3%	42	+4.4%
1947	170	−6.3%	107	+15.1%	4.3	73	−9.2%	47	+11.6%

Year	Equity Price Index December		Equity Income Index December		Income Yield %	Equity Price Index Adjusted for Cost of Living		Equity Income Index Adjusted for Cost of Living	
1948	157	−7.7%	98	−7.7%	4.3	64	−12.1%	41	−12.1%
1949	141	−10.3%	103	+4.4%	5.0	55	−13.3%	42	+0.8%
1950	149	+5.6%	109	+5.6%	5.0	57	+2.3%	43	+2.3%
1951	153	+3.0%	121	+11.2%	5.4	52	−8.1%	42	−0.7%
1952	144	−5.9%	128	+6.3%	6.1	46	−11.5%	42	−0.0%
1953	170	+17.8%	134	+4.3%	5.4	54	+16.6%	44	+3.2%
1954	242	+42.4%	155	+16.0%	4.4	74	+36.9%	49	+11.6%
1955	256	+5.8%	179	+15.4%	4.8	74	−0.0%	53	+9.1%
1956	220	−13.9%	183	+2.2%	5.7	62	−16.5%	53	−0.8%
1957	205	−7.0%	188	+2.8%	6.3	55	−11.1%	52	−1.7%
1958	289	+41.1%	202	+7.5%	4.8	76	+38.5%	55	+5.5%
1959	432	+49.5%	227	+12.1%	3.6	113	+49.5%	61	+12.1%
1960	421	−2.6%	276	+21.7%	4.5	108	−4.4%	73	+19.5%
1961	409	−3.0%	286	+3.5%	4.8	101	−7.0%	73	−0.8%
1962	391	−4.4%	285	−0.4%	5.0	94	−6.9%	71	−3.0%
1963	450	+15.2%	266	−6.5%	4.1	106	+13.1%	65	−8.2%
1964	405	−10.0%	303	+13.7%	5.1	91	−14.2%	70	+8.5%
1965	428	+5.9%	326	+7.7%	5.2	92	+1.3%	73	+3.1%
1966	389	−9.3%	328	+0.5%	5.8	81	−12.5%	70	−3.1%
1967	500	+28.7%	319	−2.5%	4.4	101	+25.6%	67	−4.8%
1968	718	+43.5%	339	+6.1%	3.2	137	+35.4%	67	+0.2%
1969	609	−15.2%	342	+0.8%	3.9	111	−19.0%	65	−3.7%
1970	563	−7.5%	360	+5.5%	4.4	95	−14.3%	63	−2.3%
1971	799	+41.9%	379	+5.1%	3.3	124	+30.2%	61	−3.6%
1972	901	+12.8%	414	+9.3%	3.2	130	+4.8%	62	+1.6%
1973	619	−31.4%	430	+3.9%	4.8	81	−37.9%	58	−6.0%

Year	Equity Price Index December		Equity Income Index December		Income Yield %	Equity Price Index Adjusted for Cost of Living		Equity Income Index Adjusted for Cost of Living	
1974	276	−55.3%	472	+9.6%	11.7	30	−62.5%	53	−8.0%
1975	653	+136.3%	521	+10.4%	5.5	57	+89.2%	47	−11.6%
1976	628	−3.9%	588	+12.8%	6.4	48	−16.5%	46	−2.0%
1977	886	+41.2%	682	+16.1%	5.3	60	+25.9%	48	+3.5%
1978	910	+2.7%	768	+12.6%	5.8	57	−5.3%	50	+3.9%
1979	949	+4.3%	951	+23.8%	6.9	51	−11.0%	53	+5.6%
1980	1206	+27.1%	1073	+12.8%	6.1	56	+10.4%	52	−2.0%
1981	1294	+7.2%	1111	+3.5%	5.9	54	−4.3%	48	−7.6%
1982	1579	+22.1%	1211	+9.0%	5.3	62	+15.8%	49	+3.4%
1983	1944	+23.1%	1309	+8.1%	4.6	73	+16.9%	51	+2.7%
1984	2450	+26.0%	1578	+20.6%	4.4	88	+20.5%	58	+15.3%
1985	2822	+15.2%	1781	+12.8%	4.3	95	+9.0%	62	+6.8%
1986	3452	+22.3%	2033	+14.1%	4.0	112	+17.9%	68	+10.0%
1987	3596	+4.2%	2264	+11.4%	4.3	113	+0.4%	74	+7.4%
1988	3829	+6.5%	2628	+16.1%	4.7	113	−0.3%	80	+8.7%
1989	4978	+30.0%	3076	+17.0%	4.2	136	+20.7%	87	+8.7%
1990	4265	−14.3%	3401	+10.5%	5.5	107	−21.6%	88	+1.1%
1991	4907	+15.1%	3591	+5.6%	5.0	117	+10.1%	89	+1.1%
1992	5635	+14.8%	3573	−0.5%	4.4	131	+11.9%	86	−3.0%
1993	6951	+23.3%	3414	−4.4%	3.4	159	+21.0%	81	−6.2%
1994	6286	−9.6%	3684	+7.9%	4.0	140	−12.1%	85	+4.9%
1995	7450	+18.5%	4127	+12.0%	3.8	161	+14.8%	92	+8.5%
1996	8320	+11.7%	4536	+9.9%	3.7	175	+9.0%	99	+7.3%
1997	9962	+19.7%	4690	+3.4%	3.2	202	+15.5%	98	−0.2%
1998	11048	+10.9%	4026	−14.2%	2.5	218	+7.9%	82	−16.5%
1999	13396	+21.20%	4140	+2.8%	2.1	260	+19.1%	83	+1.0%
2000	12329	−8.0%	4007	−3.2%	2.2	233	−10.6%	78	−5.9%

Appendix B

Names and Addresses of Charities and Other Relevant Organizations

Charities

1. Abbeyfield Cheam Society Ltd
   'Mingulay'
   17 Higher Drive
   Banstead
   Surrey
   SM7 1PL   Tel.: 020 - 8786 8280

2. Arthritis Research Council
   Copeman House
   St Mary's Gate
   Chesterfield
   Derbyshire
   S41 7TD   Tel.: 01246 - 855033

3. Barnardo's
   Tanners Lane
   Barkingside
   Ilford
   Essex
   IG6 1QG   Tel.: 020 - 8550 8822

4. British Federation of Women Graduates
   Charitable Foundation
   28 Great James Street
   London
   WC1N 3EY   Tel. 020 - 7404 6447

5. Charities Aid Foundation
   Kings Hill
   West Malling
   Kent
   ME19 4TA   Tel.: 01732 - 520000

6. Hearing Dogs for Deaf People
   London Road (A40)
   Lewknor
   Oxford
   OX49 5RY   Tel.: 01844 - 353898

7. Imperial War Museum
   Lambeth Road
   Southwark
   London SE1 6HZ   Tel.: 020 - 7416 5000

8. King George's Fund for Sailors
   8 Hatherley Street
   London SW1P 2YY   Tel.: 020 - 7932 0000

9. Ralph Snow Charity
   c/o W.B. Rymer
   Streeter Marshall
   74 High Steet
   Croydon
   Surrey
   CR9 2LU   Tel.: 020 - 8680 2638

10. Royal Agricultural Benevolent Institution
    Shaw House
    27 West Way
    Botley
    Oxford
    OX2 0QH   Tel.: 01865 - 724931

11. Royal Association for Disability and Rehabilitation (Radar)
    12 City Forum
    250 City Road
    London
    EC1V 8AF   Tel.: 020 - 7250 3222

12. Royal Air Force Pathfinder Museum
    RAF Wyton
    Huntingdonshire   Tel.: 01480 - 52451 - Ext 7493

13. Royal College of Radiologists
    32 Portland Place
    London
    W1N 3DG   Tel.: 020 - 7636 4432

14. Royal Marines Association
    Eastney Parade
    Southsea
    Hants.
    PO4 9PX   Tel.: 023 - 9273 1978

15. Royal Marines Corps Funds
    (including Royal Marines Benevolent Fund)
    H.Q. Royal Marines
    HMS *Excellent*
    Whale Island
    Portsmouth
    Hants.
    PO2 8ER   Tel.: 023 - 9265 1304

16. Royal Marines Museum
    Eastney Parade
    Southsea
    Hants
    PO4 9PX   Tel.: 023 - 9281 9385

17. RN and RM Dependent Relatives Fund
    c/o P.H. Wallis
    Centurion Building
    Grange Road
    Gosport
    Hants
    PO13 9XA   Tel.: 023 - 9270 2101

18. Spastics Society (now Scope)
    6 Market Road
    London
    N7 9PW   Tel.: 020 - 7619 7100

19. SSAFA Forces Help
    19 Queen Elizabeth Street
    London
    SE1 2LP   Tel.: 020 - 7403 8783

20. Worshipful Company of Turners
    Room 182/3
    3-7 Temple Chambers
    Temple Avenue
    London
    EC4Y 0HP   Tel.: 020 - 7353 9595

Addresses of Other Relevant Associations etc.

1. Association of Investment Trust Companies
   8 Chiswell Street
   London
   EC1Y 4YY   Tel.: 020 - 7282 5555

2. Association of Unit Trusts
   65 Kingsway
   London
   WC2B 6TD   Tel.: 020 - 7831 0898

3. Charity Commission
   Harmsworth House
   13/15 Bouverie Street
   London
   EC4Y 8DP   Tel.: 0870 - 333 0123

4. Chartered Institute of Management Accountants
   63 Portland Place
   London
   W1B 1AB   Tel.: 020 - 7637 2311

5. Barclays Capital
   5 The North Colonnade
   Canary Wharf
   London
   E14 4BB   Tel.: 020 - 7623 2323